Manchester
oddities

Manchester oddities

Curious people and places
around Manchester

KEITH WARRENDER

Willow
PUBLISHING

Old mark of the Manchester Fire Insurance
Company on a cottage at Rostherne.

Text copyright ©Keith Warrender 2011
Photographs ©Keith Warrender 2011 unless acknowledged
First published 2011 by Willow Publishing

Willow Publishing
36 Moss Lane, Timperley
Altrincham, Cheshire WA15 6SZ

ISBN 978-0-946361-43-4

Book designed by Keith Warrender
Printed by the Buxton Press

Dedicated to my wife Judith

Cover: White Nancy, Bollington
Opposite title page: The Pigeon Tower, Rivington
Title page: Veiled lady, Booth Street, Manchester

Contents

*places marked with an asterisk are outside
the borough boundaries but are included
in the section.

Black knight sculpture, Council Offices Wellington Road, Ashton (see page 63)

Pillbox from the last War on the south side of Rochdale Road East, near Heywood Cemetery.

Introduction

Oddities come in many different forms. They may be forgotten things that were once commonplace. It is the unusual and the unique - the first, the largest the only, etc. Architectural follies and wayside memorials are also my idea of oddities, as are some of the eccentric characters from the past. Many of the towers, caves and castles are the fantasy creations of rich industrialists. These are people and places to enjoy and to celebrate in a sometimes bland world.

The book covers an area within about twenty miles from the centre of Manchester, but if there was something worthy of inclusion nearby I have gone beyond. Please note the places outside the Greater Manchester area boundaries are grouped with the nearest borough.

This is just a selection of the curiosities - I am aware of others. If you know of something which could be included in a later publication, please contact me.

I would encourage you to see these places for yourself wherever possible, but check websites for the latest information on opening times and access. Please respect the privacy of the owners of oddities on private property. Unless permission is granted, the public are not allowed in their grounds.

The book is a great resource for places to visit, and a reminder of the beautiful countryside and the fascinating communities around the region. I hope you have as much enjoyment reading it, as I've had researching the subject, taking photographs and being helped by many people.

Keith Warrender
Timperley 2011

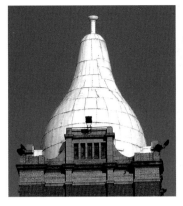  

L to R: Pear Mill Stockport,
Cat on building near junction of Gatley
Road and Wilmslow Road Cheadle,
Building on Whitelands Road Ashton,
Fire watchers tower on the Warrington
transporter bridge

Stacksteads   Bacup

Rawtenstall
Stubbins

Turton

Rivington

Bury

Rochdale

Oldham

Bolton

Wigan   Salford   Manchester   Tameside

Tintwistle

Robin Hood's
Picking Rods

Trafford   Stockport

Warrington

Lymm

Rostherne
Bucklow Hill
Arley   Tatton Park
Tabley   Knutsford

Styal
Wilmslow   Adlington   Bollington
Prestbury
Rainow

What more could you want? A cottage at Hollingworth
which is both sunny and financially secure.

MANCHESTER

Alpine roof figures

Two sitting figures can be seen at the top of Caxton's Buildings at 77-83 Piccadilly. They appear to be part of the 'Alpine' style of the upper storey of the building designed by architects Clegg and Knowles in 1877. The figure fronting onto Piccadilly seems to be holding a dog. Prominent gargoyles and sculptures did not usually feature in their work, and there has been speculation that they were later additions. There is also a dragon carving on the roof which is hidden from view at pavement level.

Caxton's Buildings, Piccadilly

The figures had been badly eroded by the early 1990s and were rebuilt. The dragon was completely re-made in sandstone. The architects' work is to be seen throughout the city centre. They had offices at Brown Street, later moving to Cross Street, Manchester.

John Knowles came from Somerset, and lived at Park Place off Cheetham Hill Road. Charles Clegg was Manchester born and lived at 'Linden Lea', Brooklands Road, Sale. Charles, who also designed the Imperial Hotel in Blackpool, died in 1922 at the age of ninety-three.

Grocers Warehouse tunnel

This mysterious waterway off the Rochdale Canal near Deansgate is the remains of the Grocers' Warehouse tunnel. Boats passed through the warehouse (which has been partially reconstructed) into the cliff tunnel where the goods were winched up, close to Bridgewater Street. Some have thought that the tunnel extended much further towards the cathedral but there is no evidence of this. The Rochdale canal was built after the tunnel.

City Pub

The pub, on Oldham Street, previously known as the Prince of Orange has this plasterwork carving depicting William and Mary arriving in England, welcomed by Britannia, a clergyman, two helmeted women and an angel with trumpets. The Dutch Protestant, William, took over the throne from Catholic King James II in 1689. The pub was popular with the traders from the nearby Smithfield Market when it was in the City centre.

William Marsden's Saturday 'Half holiday'

Many look forward to the weekend to be away from work but, within living memory, people in offices and factories worked on Saturday mornings. The five and a half day working week was the norm, and until the 1840s it would have been all day Saturday.

From around 1837 some businesses were already enjoying half-day working on either Fridays or Saturdays, but it was not a widely accepted practice. This encouraged others to seek the same working hours. Thanks to the campaigning of a committee chaired by William Marsden, four hundred and forty one Manchester businesses, in November 1843, agreed to this concession, despite vigorous opposition from mill owners. Some feared that young men would 'misapply the time they had in hand on the Saturday afternoon' when the mills and warehouses closed at 1pm, but naturally the working population gratefully accepted this new freedom which was later adopted nationally.

St John's Gardens
Byrom Street

Over six hundred were invited to a celebration of the new 'weekly half holiday' at Manchester Town Hall which was then in King Street. Marsden, the son of a linen and cotton manufacturer, was only twenty three when he became the chairman of the committee and died five years later. Marsden was ably assisted by Robert Jacques Lowes who was the honorary secretary to the committee, and led the 25th anniversary celebrations in 1868.

William Marsden's portrait was later on display in the entrance to the Free Library on King Street. He was buried at St John's Church on Byrom Street and his name is now on a memorial in the gardens where 22,000 people were laid to rest.

Shakespearian comedy

The merry figures are on the frontage of the Shakespeare pub, Fountain Street off Market Street. There has been a tavern on this site since 1771 but the present building is said to have been taken down from its original site in Chester and re-erected in Manchester in 1928.

Mysterious dome

This dome has stood in a front garden just off Mauldeth Road in Whalley Range for over ten years and must have puzzled many passers-by. It is part of an observatory which once stood in the grounds of a house in Bowdon. It belonged to Alfred Gaddum, who was a Fellow of the Royal Astronomical Society, and died in 1954. The Gaddum family were well-known as wealthy industrialists but also for their philanthropy. Besides being chairman of a company of Manchester silk merchants, Alfred gave much support to Ancoats Hospital. He met his future wife there when she was a matron. Harry, his brother, was founder of the pioneering Gaddum House where many charitable organisations were based.

The street with no name

Over the years the street at the side of Levenshulme station had inexplicably been left unnamed and is known by locals as 'The Street With No Name'. A sign bearing this name was erected in 2007. When this disappeared Northern Trains agreed to put up a larger sign out of harm's way. The station platform signs are unusual because they are in several languages.

Rose Hill - home of the 'Shar-stone' and the 'Icebergs'

In the grounds of Ashley Grange there is a huge glacial boulder known as the 'Shar-stone' brought from Woodhouse farm in 1892. The property once known as Rose Hill was the home of Sir Edward Watkin (1819-1901) described as 'The Second Railway King'. Like his predecessor, George Hudson, Watkin was involved in many railway projects around the world including the Canadian Pacific. Distinguished friends came to visit him at Rose Hill including statesmen Benjamin Disraeli and William Gladstone, and Charles Dickens. He was among the VIPs on the first trip on board Stephenson's Rocket locomotive. By 2003 the house was in danger of demolition but it has been renovated and expanded into apartments.

The stone at Ashley Grange, off Bronington Close, Northenden

Watkin was involved in several high profile failures including the first attempt to build a railway tunnel under the Channel in 1875. Two miles into the project, it was abandoned over fears of invasion by France. A mob surrounded Watkin's London home and smashed the windows. He had also envisaged an underground rail link between Scotland and Ireland.

Watkins was also an MP and represented Great Yarmouth, Stockport and Hythe. In 1894 he was involved in a project to build a tower taller than the 'Eiffel' in Paris at Wembley Park, London. Gustave Eiffel was invited to design it but declined because he decided it would be unpatriotic to be part of a rival scheme. A 500-guineas prize was offered by Watkin for the best design. The winning tower was around 150ft taller than its Parisian counterpart and would have been the world's tallest structure. The judging committee were disappointed that none of the entries had been outstanding. Steel for the tower came from Newton Heath Ironworks, and Heenan and Froude, a Manchester company who had previously built Blackpool Tower, were awarded the contract to erect the steelwork.

Below right: A fanciful entry
in the competition for the new
tower design, which would
travel between the countries.

Below: A comparison between
the English and French towers.

The pleasure gardens opened in May 1894 and visitors were able to
see the almost-completed first section of the tower. Work up to the
first platform where shops, restaurants, Turkish baths and a theatre
were planned, was finished the following year. However, work on
the tower stopped at this point because of insufficient funding, and
problems with subsidence which caused the tower to tilt. By around
1902 the tower was closed because of its declining condition.

In 1906 it was announced by the Wembley Tower Company that the
tower, which had been 'a lamentable failure from the first', was to
be pulled down. In September 1907, the final leg of the tower was
brought down with explosives and was heard all over northwest
London. The scrap metal was taken to Italy, and the site used for the
1924 British Empire Exhibition, and later for Wembley Stadium.

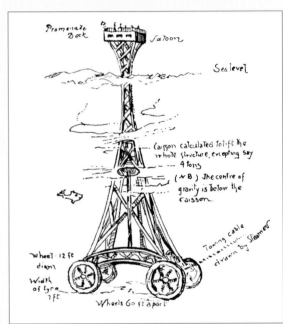

Watkin purchased a painting
entitled 'The Icebergs' by American
painter Frederick Church for around
£10,000. After Watkin's death in 1901 it
remained on the property during the
time it was used as a hospital, orphan-
age and remand home. However, it was
sold at auction for £2 million to the
Dallas Museum of Fine Arts to raise
money for a gym at the remand home.
The gym was demolished in 1985.

THE TOWER AT WEMBLEY AS IT WILL BE WHEN COMPLETE

THE EIFFEL TOWER

Time gentlemen ...

The report of Manchester's Building and Sanitary Committee in 1851 stated that they had constructed sixty-nine urinals next to pubs and beerhouses. There were three other public urinals including one on Great Ancoats Street. The first flushing public toilet appeared in London in 1852, but there was none in Manchester until the early 1990s, in Piccadilly and Albert Square. Urinals such as this one at Charles Street next to the Lass 'o' Gowrie with its outlet direct into the river, had been phased out by the 1890s. By the late 1930s, the city had 145 public conveniences. Only 31 were for females because it was thought in years gone by that women should not be wandering the streets. With present expenditure cuts, publicly-owned toilets may again become rare.

The veiled lady

This unusual carving is on the frontage of the Renaissance-style Massey Chambers, Booth Street, close to Albert Square, by Manchester architect Edward Salomons in 1872. Salomons also designed the striking Reform Club on King Street. The theme gave an opportunity for the sculptor to demonstrate his skill in depicting the veiled Renaissance woman.

Decorative directions

Surely the most ornate signs in the city for Hanover Street and Liberation Street, on buildings owned by the Cooperative Society.

'Scutch Buttock'

This is one of the more unusual names in the region, referring to two cottages in Newton Heath. It was the home of a coachman at Culcheth Hall who it was said, would threaten to 'scutch' or whip the horses, if they were restive. The name for the cottages was in official use because it is on the 1848 Ordnance Survey map and was referred to in February 1880 when the local board of health were inviting tenders to build a sewer from 'Scutch Buttock to Culcheth Gates'.

Greengrocer's saint

The statue of St George and the dragon is set into the wall belonging to Evans the greengrocers near the corner of Barlow Moor Road and Didsbury Road. It was put there by the previous owner in the early 1970s during improvements to the shop frontage. It had cost £25 from a local firm of monumental masons at Elm House, Didsbury. The statue is made from Cumberland marble which is known for its hardness. It was made for a church but they could not afford to buy it, and it was left in the sculptors' garden. The sculptors' business ended when one of the brothers who owned it died from the occupational hazard of inhaling stone dust.

Manchester's Civil Justice Centre, Crown Square, shows that curiosities are not entirely things from the past. Some have likened the building to filing cabinet drawers and a container terminal. It is nonetheless an impressive structure.

Temple Folly

The Temple folly in Heaton Park stands on Manchester's highest point. It was designed by the eminent architect James Wyatt for Sir Thomas Egerton, around 1800. Egerton was a man of many pursuits and interests, including science and astronomy. He bought a telescope in 1803 and is thought to have used the building as an observatory. Note the top of the dome, which is a scaled-down version of the temple. The building was nearly demolished in 1963 because of the need for £1550 of roof repairs.

Circus Tavern

The pub on Portland Street is thought to be the smallest in Manchester - with just two rooms and space for only one person behind the bar. To avoid congestion at peak times, customers are asked to find a seat and they are served from there.

Its name comes from a circus hall in nearby Chatham Street, built in 1793. The venture was not a commercial success and tragically ended when the circus troupe drowned on a voyage to Ireland. Travelling circuses often stopped in the Portland Street area and entertainers and customers would drop in here and at other drinking establishments. The tavern dates from around 1790.

The grained partitions are said to be over a hundred years old. On the walls are photographs of celebrities who have visited this small but friendly pub.

Bomb survivor

The post box is a symbol of Manchester's resilience and resurgence after the terrorist bomb on 15 June 1996 which did so much damage in that part of the city centre. The post box remained almost undamaged during the blast and was returned to its original position on Corporaton Street in 1999 once the redevelopment work was completed.

Green watch

This green man carving over a newsagents near the junction of Cross Street and Albert Square keeps a rather sinister watch over people crossing the road.

Sam Scott - river jumper

The noted American river jumper came to Manchester in 1837. It might be inferred from his title that he would jump over water, however he specialised in jumping into water from great heights - a skill he had developed while serving in the American navy. The previous week he had been leaping from mast-heads of vessels in Liverpool. A crowd assembled to watch him jump from a six-storey warehouse near Bridge Street, into the River Irwell.

He appeared on the roof wearing a red shirt, lace trousers and a swimming cap tied by strings round the throat and asked the crowd to give generously. Next he ran across the slate roof and plunged feet first into the murky river. Moments later he returned to the surface holding stones taken from the river bed. Afterwards he announced he would make a second jump later that day, this time diving head first. An even bigger crowd witnessed this feat and he swam back to the river bank to great cheers. He collected no more than £3 for his two efforts. Scott then continued on his tour of the country, including Bolton where the police stopped him after his first dive, and a plunge from a forty-foot high cliff in Cornwall.

Tragically he died during one of his stunts on Waterloo Bridge London in 1841. He would pretend to hang himself and writhe around on gallows by the side of the bridge before plunging into the water.

On this day, the trick went horribly wrong and the noose must have been in the wrong position. Friends and onlookers thought he was just acting and left him there for three minutes before they cut him down. He was taken to Charing Cross Hospital where they unsucessfully tried to revive him. Ironically the hanging trick had nearly gone wrong the previous year but he had survived that. He was twenty-seven at the time of his death.

Moss's Folly

Etrop Grange hotel on Thorley Lane, near Manchester Airport, was once a private residence known locally in the 18th century as 'Moss's Folly'. Passers-by were amazed to see the owner, William Moss, eating at a table accompanied by several wax models. The figure at the top of the table was addressed as 'Mrs Moss'. Perhaps his wife had died and he coped with his loneliness by bringing in the silent female guests. It fooled visitors to the district who, on seeing the assembled diners through the window, would bow and raise their hats in polite greeting.

Curiosities around Styal

Robert Hyde Gregg lived at Norcliffe Hall. He travelled around the world with his father on commercial trips and became interested in ancient sites and is thought to have built the stone circle and the mock ruined folly in the 1850s.

(The grounds of the hall are privately owned and are not open to the public.)

Above: Stone circle

Far left: Obelisk in a field close to the car park thought to be directly in line with the sun at noon from an old observatory built by the Greggs.

Left: Folly ruins in the grounds of Norcliffe Hall.

Below: Norcliffe Hall

Romany's caravan

'Romany' was the name thought up by George Bramwell Evens for his weekly broadcasts of countryside rambles which were popular with children and adults. He was a Methodist minister and the nephew of Gipsy Cornelius Smith, a preacher and gospel-singer. His knowledge of the countryside was self-taught and he thought that it was his gipsy ancestry that made him a roamer and a lover of the countryside.

He had bought the caravan, or 'vardo' as it is known in Romany, in 1921 for £75 at a fair in Cumbria and used it for family holidays. Under the name of 'The Tramp', he wrote a series of newspaper nature articles which were to provide the inspiration for the BBC programmes.

Broadcasts of nature rambles 'Out With Romany' on Children's Hour with Raq his dog, Comma (so named because she never came to a full stop), his horse, and two young friends, Doris and Muriel, began in Manchester in 1932 and later nationally in 1938.

The realism of the sound effects and his vivid accounts of country life gave the impression they were actually recording spontaneously in the countryside. When it emerged in a Radio Times article that the programme was made live in a studio, some readers complained they had been deceived by the BBC. He was credited with a number of Romany books, and also wrote under the name of 'The Tramp'.

When he died in November 1943, such was Bramwell Even's popularity that many children were shocked and lessons had to be cancelled. The BBC was flooded with messages of condolence for the pioneering naturalist who used to attract 13 million listeners. There was a memorial service at the Albert Hall for Evens who was regarded as one of the BBC's finest broadcasters.

The caravan was parked in its present position in 1944 in his home town of Wilmslow. He moved there in 1939 after ill-health caused him to retire from the ministry. The caravan is said to be the smallest tourist attraction in the country. There is also a headstone here where his dog Raq is buried.

Terry Waite, patron of the Romany Society founded in 1943, claimed that during his captivity in Beirut it was memories of the Romany broadcasts that helped him through the ordeal. The caravan with its original contents is open to the public on some Saturdays in the summer.

Above: Toy windmill made by Evens

Middle: Paints in the caravan, used by Bramwell Evens

Top: Romany's caravan, Wilmslow

Inset: Bramwell Evens and Raq

Teetotal Sampson

'Sampson' was a regular at the Knott Mill and Salford fairs, at New Cross and Stevenson Square in Manchester performing many feats of strength. He was five feet nine inches tall, and quite slim and yet able to lift heavy men and sacks of coal above his head and break or bend iron bars and chains. In another stunt he would lie on his back with a heavy stone on his chest which was then broken by burly men with sledge hammers. Accompanied by his daughter who was also a weight lifter, 'Sampson' juggled with fifty-six pound weights and pulled coal carts and lorries. He had been seen to lift a lorry on his shoulders. His Biblical nickname came from his hair which hung down almost to his waist, and from his dedication to the Temperance movement, giving many lectures on the subject. At the start of his feats, he always gave a short speech about the benefits of refraining from alcohol. He headed the annual temperance procession on Whit Monday riding a horse, and attributed his strength to his training and no doubt his abstinence. His real name was J Johnson and he was a carter.

Styal cave

The cave is situated in the 'picturesque' garden created by mill-owner Samuel Greg and his wife Hannah at Quarry Bank. It is thought to be partly natural with some stone quarried out to be used either for the mill or their house.

There are accounts of use being made of other caves next to the river Bollin. Samuel Finney in his 1785 survey of Wilmslow suggested a family had lived there, while others talk of its being the home of Disley, a hermit. The caves may have been a temporary resting place for traders on their way to the salt mines or to the Yorkshire woollen manufacturers. There is also mention of its being used by a blacksmith. Old photographs show the caves were used by Greg as a boathouse and also for the dam's sluice machinery.

RULES AND REGULATIONS

TO BE OBSERVED BY

The Members of the Hen-Peck'd Club,

HELD AT THE HOUSE OF Mr. JAMES BARNISH,

HARK UP TO GLORY, ST. MARY'S GATE, ROCHDALE.

Come all you Young Men who have never been dubb'd,
You may now have a chance at the Hen-Peck'd Club.

1. That every member of this society shall kindle the fire, set the kettle over, and have the water boiling before he awakes his wife in the morning.

2. That every member shall take his wife her clothes to bed, after having aired and made them warm and comfortable, or be fined twopence for each offence

3. That he shall state to his wife the work he has done, and ask if there is anything more she wishes him to perform before he goes to his work in the morning.

4. That if any member or members should come home to his dinner, and find his wife gossiping and the dinner not ready, he shall not complain; but cook for himself and family, and something for his wife that will make her comfortable when she does come home, or forfeit threepence.

5. That if any member or members after their day's labour come home and find that his wife has not washed the pots, or any other thing he thinks should have been done, he must do the same himself, and not find fault; he must likewise mend the fire, warm the water, sweep the house, mop and scrub the floor, and then make the bed or beds to her satisfaction, or forfeit fourpence.

6. That when any member shall have finished his week's work, he shall return home with his wages and give the same to his wife.

7. That when any member has given the wages to his wife, he shall ask her what she wishes him to do the next, if she wishes him to go to the shop he must go, but if she wish to go herself he must stay at home to clean the house and furniture, and set things in order, that she may be satisfied when she returns, or forfeit sixpence.

8. That every Sunday morning, each member shall rise at six o'clock, kindle the fire, clean and dress the children (if any) and get them ready for school, before his beloved wife shall be disturbed; but if she call for a pipe of tobacco, a pinch of snuff, or a glass of some nourishing cordial, he shall serve her that instant, or forfeit sixpence.

9. That peradventure a member's wife may wish to have some splendid clothing such as a silk velvet bonnet, a fine cap with artificials, a new gown, crinoline, boots, sandals, silk stockings, or any other article of fashionable dress, her husband shall provide for such things out of his over-time money, or forfeit one shilling and eightpence.

10. That when a member's wife is sick or in labour, he shall run for the doctor as fast as he can, whether it be night or day, frost or snow, hail or rain, or forfeit two shillings.

11. That any member refusing to clean the child when it has shitten or bawed (as the term may be), he shall forfeit sixpence.

12. That every member shall wash the child's shitten hippins, when his wife orders him, or forfeit fourpence.

13. That every Monday night, each member shall clean his wife and children's shoes and clogs.

14. That every Tuesday night each member shall look up the clothes for washing.

15. That every Wednesday night each member shall look the buttery over, and see whether there be a sufficient quantity of tea, coffee, sugar, butter, bread, cheese, meal, flour, beef or mutton, and if found wanting, he shall provide the same without grumbling.

16. That every Thursday night, each member shall provide for his loving wife such things as may improve her private happiness, such as cordials or spirits, according to circumstances.

17. That every Friday night, each member shall look up the stockings, shirts, &c., and such as want mending he shall mend them.

18. That every member shall pay the strictest observance to the five last-named rules or forfeit threepence for every neglect on conviction before the committee.

19. That the entrance fee shall be fourpence for each member.

20. That the anniversary shall be held on the day called Good Friday in each year.

21. That any young man or bachelor intending to be married within two months from the time he enters, may be admitted by paying sixpence.

22. That each and every member pay twopence per month, to go to the fund.

23. That all fines and forfeitures go to the fund.

24. That the relief be granted in the following manner:—To every member who may have received from his loving wife, without any just cause or provocation, One black eye .... 1s. 6d. per week.
Two ditto .... 2s. 9d. do.
Two ditto with scratched } nose .... } 4s. 3d. do.
One black eye with } scratched face on } 4s. 6d. do. both sides .... }
One or more teeth knocked } 1s. 2d. per week for out................. } life.

Signed on behalf of the Society,

JOHNNY OBEY-THY-WIFE.

See page 35

The tower off Stubbins Vale Road.

The 'Wet Tower'

The tower was also known as the 'Tentering' or 'Drying' Tower because of its former use for drying woollen cloth, which was hung from the top storey and then smoked or fumigated with sulphur candles. It was built in 1866 above Stubbins Vale Mill, and owned by the Porritt brothers who had houses for themselves and their workers in the hamlet. The 'Wet Tower' was originally single storey but was later developed into the present-day 'eye-catcher'.

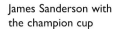
James Sanderson with the champion cup

'Treacle' the champion pedestrian

Whitworth blacksmith, James 'Treacle' Sanderson achieved national fame as an athlete, winning several national titles in the 1860s. The nickname of 'Treacle' comes from his father, who enjoyed treacle on his bread. This must have been unusual because locals subsequently called all the Sanderson family and their descendants by this name.

'Treacle' was one of the most noted athletes or 'pedestrians' as they were known at that time. His first big achievement was to win the mile and a half champion cup at Stockport in 1862.

The following year, he was victorious in the one and a quarter-mile champion cup at Sheffield, and then the four mile championships in London. His greatest race during that momentous year, was his narrow defeat to William Lang 'the Crow-catcher' in a two mile race at the City Grounds, Bradford in Manchester. Sanderson, using his usual tactic, took an early lead and set a fast pace establishing a six yard gap. Lang gradually got back into contention and in an exciting finish he was first over the line with Sanderson just one second behind.

Above: The track beside
Cowm Reservoir where
Treacle did his speed training.

Right: His home at Foldhead.

The winning time was nine seconds inside the previous record, and it was not to be beaten by anyone for almost forty years. In 1876, in his late thirties, 'Treacle' twice beat London's champion runner George Hazel, who was nine years his junior, over four miles.

Sanderson was born in 1837, the son of a blacksmith, and by his teens the enjoyment of running on the moors had made him into a promising athlete. At the age of eighteen he won races at the annual carnival at Lobden, near Whitworth, and in May 1858 he won £1 for running a mile in five minutes on the Whitworth Road. Over the next four years he established himself as a leading runner, winning many races at the Copenhagen Grounds, at Newton Heath, Manchester.

'Pedestrianism' was a professional sport with betting taking place at the events. Races were arranged by promoters and the tracks were usually on property adjoining pubs. The Royal Oak Grounds, at Newton Heath in Manchester, was one of the biggest venues in the country, and there was a crowd of 20,000 to watch 'Treacle' (or 'Traykle' as it is pronounced in Whitworth) come second to Lang in the opening meeting there in 1864. The site was over 17 acres, with a grandstand for 2000 and a circular running track with each quarter mile marked by a coloured flag. Such was the anticipation at this event, large crowds gathering early, broke though barriers and got in free with a number of people crushed.

The pedestrians would put up the prize money and in unofficial national championships they also received cups or belts. Generally they would race for a minimum of '£25 a-side'. If they beat off all challengers over a year, they would be awarded a valuable silver or gold cup. 'Treacle' Sanderson, also billed as 'The Whitworth Flyer' and 'Rap from Cowcliff' raced at Hyde Park in Sheffield and at Bow and Hackney Wick in London.

The stables next to the house, where 'Treacle' had his sauna.

It was after one of the races in Sheffield that thieves tried to steal his prize money. Perhaps they were picking on the wrong person in attempting to rob a long-distance athlete. Possibly they thought he would be exhausted after his race, and they gave chase to 'Treacle'. He was wearing clogs as he reputedly ran and walked all the way back across the Pennines from Sheffield to Whitworth and managed to keep ahead of them. By the time he reached home, when his family helped him to take off his clogs, his feet were covered in blood.

At five feet seven inches tall and around eight stone and ten pounds in weight, he was slight in build. He was a dedicated athlete and trained regularly around the moors of the neighbourhood and practised speed training on the road by Cowm Reservoir. Sanderson timed himself over 440 yards between the waterworks gate and a mark he had carved on the reservoir stone wall. Many years later part of the wall was demolished but the mark has been preserved.

'Treacle' adhered to a strict diet of mutton, potatoes, bread and a glass of ale at lunch, followed by fresh eggs and two cups of tea for his evening meal. This special diet had been recommended by his friend Dr James Eastwood Taylor - the last of the Whitworth 'bone-setters'. Sanderson also set up a sauna in his smithy where he would sit, sweating under blankets, to lose weight. The Sanderson family are said to have Scottish ancestry and came to settle in Whitworth during the 1745 Jacobite Rebellion. James inherited his ancestors' athleticism as they kept themselves ready for battle with races, tournaments and games.

In his last competitive race in 1877 he was beaten in the four miles by McLeavy in Glasgow. Sanderson was proud that he had beaten all his main rivals over the years, with the exception of Scottish Champion Robert Mc-Kinstray, who was twenty-one while he was coming to the end of his career at the age of thirty-nine. Sanderson's record was impressive - out of around fifty-six races over twenty one years, he had won twenty-nine.

'Treacle' retired from active competition and concentrated on exhibition runs. Throughout most of his career as a 'pedestrian' he had continued working as a master blacksmith at the local quarry belonging to Heyes and Company, making and sharpening tools. However, between 1862 and 1865, when he was at his peak, he seems to have raced practically full-time. In retirement he continued to have an interest in the sport. His trophies were on display at his home at Foldhead Cottages.

John Bright, the great Liberal politician and reformer was a friend and he invited Sanderson to the Houses of Parliament where the athlete drew a lot of attention. Sanderson died in 1905 one day short of sixty eight years old, survived by his widow, eight children and twenty four grandchildren.

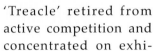

Above: The quarry where Sanderson worked.

Right: Starting pistol of the time in the ownership of Sanderson.

Below: The stones that used to be in the reservoir wall, before the section was demolished. A cross from where he timed his runs and the sprint distance are cut into the stones.

England's shortest street

Elgin Street, Bacup, was until recently the world's shortest street - just 17 feet in length. It had held the title since 1987 when it was included in the Guinness Book of Records. It still remains the shortest in England. Local historian Ken Bowden discovered that the origins of the street are difficult to trace. It is thought to date from the late 1850s but it is not seen on an Ordnance Survey map until 1893. Today the property is in an enclosed railed-off area.

The Henpecked Club

Also known as 'The Ancient Order of Henpecked Husbands', the group is said to have been in existence since 1809 when they gathered at a pub at Syke near Rochdale. They met, in theory, to escape from overbearing wives, but it was simply an excuse for an annual meal, walk or trip - usually on Easter Monday - the only day they were supposedly allowed out! The Syke club of the 'slaves to domesticity' met during the Whitworth Wakes and then walked across the moor displaying their regalia, such as fire-irons and brushes.

There have been similar groups since at Hebden Bridge, Keighley and Brighouse and they all observe a long list of rules and regulations and fines, which are not taken seriously. For example if a man had one or more teeth knocked out by his wife, he was supposed to receive 1s 2d from the Club for life. New applicants had to prove that 'on every day of the year except Easter Monday they were slaves of the apron strings and domestic drudgery'. They were asked questions such as: 'Do you bake?', 'Can you blacklead?' and 'Do you take her a cup of tea in the morning?'

The Hebden Bridge branch of the society met at chapels in remote villages to avoid publicity, although they had to endure the scornful comments of local women on their way to the meeting. More recent gatherings have been held at Brighouse, Calderdale at the local pub.

Cliffe Castle Museum at Keighley has amongst its exhibits a 'wife soothing cradle'. It was an adult-sized version of a child's wooden cradle and on the side it reads 'Henpeckd Club's peace box no.6 ....Patent cure for a cross wife'. The cradle was taken along to local events in the Keighley area. The Syke club may not have been the first because there is a Henpecked Club pamphlet published by one of its members at Workington in 1810, which suggests that the organisation had been in existence for some time. Others have claimed it is the world's oldest organisation because Adam was the first member!

Hare Hill Park folly

The folly with waterwheel and pool at Hare Hill Park, Littleborough was built during the time the property was owned by the Newall family who were big landowners in the town. The wheel was driven by a moorland stream, and until the Second World War it pumped water to the local council offices. Water was also piped to a mill from the folly. Hare Hill was bought by the council in 1901 to become a park. Nearby is also the grave of a pet monkey - Mephisto, possibly belonging to James Howard, a colliery owner, and family who were living there around that time.

Gravy Wrestling World Championships

COLIN KERRON

This curious event began in 2007 and is held at the Rose N Bowl, Stacksteads each August Bank Holiday. The contestants who step up to the plate have to wrestle for two minutes in gravy and are marked by the judges for variety of moves, fun factor and how much applause they receive. The wrestlers wear compulsory fancy dress and serious aggressiveness is penalised or even red-carded. Nevertheless, most points are awarded for pinning the opponent's shoulders down. Normally the owners of the pub restaurant supply the 440 gallons of gravy, but in 2009 Bisto generously provided a batch which was past its sell-by date.

Wrestlers come from all around the country to take part. It is a 'knockout' event and the contestants splash their way through four rounds. The winner receives an 'engravied' trophy and the proceeds of the event go to charity.

The Whitworth doctors

Around seven generations of the Taylor family provided medical help not only in Whitworth but also Todmorden, Bolton, Salford, Huddersfield and Pendle between 1700 and the late 1800s. John and George, two of the earliest and most famous doctors or bone-setters, practised at Whitworth. They were blacksmiths by trade, with no formal medical qualifications and also treated animals who were often given priority - see the cartoon below.

The doctors' reputation even reached the Royal family and John was requested to attend the Princess Royal. She had a sinus complaint which he successfully cured with snuff. Archibald Campbell Tait, who later became Archbishop of Canterbury, came to Whitworth to receive treatment for a withered leg. Of course the doctors did have their failures and in a conversation between John Taylor and Sir Charles White, one of the founders of the Manchester Infirmary, White said 'Well John, I see you're still killing people'. Taylor retorted 'Oh yes, but at a cheaper rate than you!'

People came many miles to be treated by the doctors at Whitworth. They were brought on carts, and lodged in the village where they slept on floors, sofas or in outbuildings. 'The 'Cripple's Walk' route to the doctors' cottage where

they carried out the gruesome treatment is still signposted today. The Taylors were noted for setting broken and dislocated bones, and were reputed to be able to cure those who had already sought conventional treatment. Everyone paid the same fee - 18d for medicine and attendance. The poorest didn't have to pay because the richer patients gave generously or left money in the poor box.

A black ointment, known as 'Whitworth Bottle', was made by George Taylor's wife. The ointment was boiled in a kettle and then poured onto the floor where minutes before there had been blood, skin and tissue. After the ointment had cooled, it was rolled up into sticks for the patients. Other people in the village benefited from the Taylors' service, by supplying surgical tin shoes, and whale-bone stays for spinal injuries.

Top: 'Cripples' Walk'
Above: The Doctors house, Whitworth Square
Right: The patients' residence, Whitworth Square
Below: Patients whale-bone stay

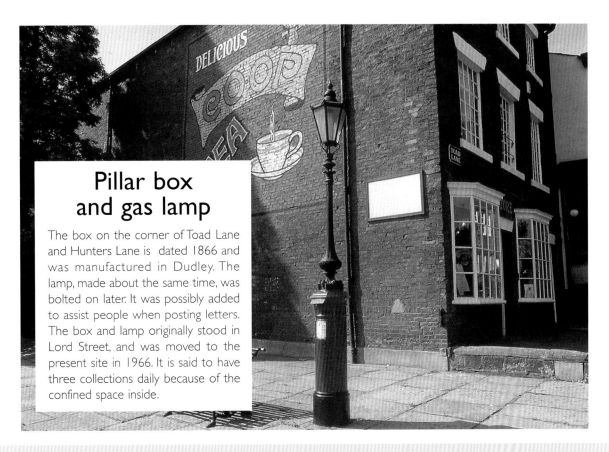

Pillar box and gas lamp

The box on the corner of Toad Lane and Hunters Lane is dated 1866 and was manufactured in Dudley. The lamp, made about the same time, was bolted on later. It was possibly added to assist people when posting letters. The box and lamp originally stood in Lord Street, and was moved to the present site in 1966. It is said to have three collections daily because of the confined space inside.

Whitworth church gargoyles

The original St Bartholomew's chapel was built in 1529 and has been rebuilt several times. Today's church was consecrated in 1850 and is notable for the gargoyles on the outside walls, some of which depict members of the congregation. One is the son of the first vicar of Whitworth, another is an old parishioner who used to spend many hours watching the stone carvers at work on the building. Over the choir vestry porch is the carving of a man who had sung in the choir for over seventy years. Above the west door on the tower is a dragon and a woman symbolising the temptation passage in the book of Genesis, and over the entrance, a guardian angel.

The Flodden window

This memorial to the battle of Flodden Field in 1513, at Middleton Parish Church, is believed to be the only stained glass war memorial of its kind in Europe. It depicts the seventeen Middleton archers led by Richard Assheton, kneeling in prayer before the bloody battle which left 8000 Scots dead and many others wounded. Each archer is named above the bow. They were among the 1,200 archers who ensured victory for England by preventing reinforcements reaching the battlefront.

Above: The marks in the church wall made by the archers

The window was installed two years later and Assheton was knighted for his valour in battle. By the 19th century the condition of the window had deteriorated and the surviving parts were re-assembled into a smaller window in the south wall of the church. Outside on the wall are the marks made by the archers as they sharpened their arrows on the stonework.

The wooden extension to the church tower, built around 1600, is thought to be one of only three in Britain. This was either to make the bells sound more pleasant, or to bear the additional weight of the bells. There was thought to be a wooden Saxon church on this site, although the present structure was largely completed in 1524 by Sir Richard Assheton.

OLDHAM

JOSEPH HOWARTH

UPWARDS OF 40 YEARS THE WELL KNOWN
BLIND BELLMAN OF OLDHAM.
ERECTED BY VOLUNTARY SUBSCRIPTIONS.
PRESENTED TO THE PARK COMMITTEE
MAY 9TH 1868.

————————

HE DIED ON THE 17TH DAY OF MAY 1862;
IN THE 76TH YEAR OF HIS AGE.

Saddleworth Rushcart

Its origins come from the tradition at Rogationtide of carrying rushes around the parish and then into church. These replaced the old rushes which had been spread onto the bare earth floors to create some insulation during the winter. By 1821 the rushes were laid up to fifteen inches deep at St Chad's Uppermill, until the local bishop complained and the practice was stopped.

Originally rushes were brought by sledge, but around 1800 in Saddleworth and other Pennine areas they came by cart and were heaped up into the shape of a haystack. The ceremony of the rush cart visiting the church continued and it developed into a festival held during the annual wakes holiday. By the early twentieth century, interest in the rushcarts had virtually died out as churches began to provide seating and heating. The 1889 Rushcart at Uppermill was in such a bad condition it had fallen apart.

The annual festival was revived in 1975 by the Saddleworth Morris Men and continues today as 'Longworth Thump', on the second weekend after August 12th. Rushes are built into a 13ft-high conical structure weighing around two tons and decorated. A different Morris Man, known as 'Jockey', sits on top each year, fortified with ale in a copper kettle and the cart is pulled by 150 invited Morris Men on the 'stangs'. On the Sunday, rushes with flowers and herbs from the cart are laid in the aisles of St Chad's. Following the service there are wrestling and gurning (funny face) competitions, and entertainment organised by the Morris Men.

Wakes curiosities

Many of the hamlets around Saddleworth had their own wakes festivals. As well as the traditional cock fighting, climbing a greasy pole and wrestling there were some more unusual pastimes.

Local writer and historian, Ammon Wrigley, described the women's sprint race at Stanedge where Moll Binn was the local champion. Running shorts were not known of, so her husband pinned her skirt and petticoat high above her knees so that she could take long strides. This naturally attracted lots of attention from locals, to see the rare sight of shapely female legs. Spectators would shout 'Poo your coats up' and 'Show yor legs' to the other runners, which they ignored. But Moll surged ahead, throwing her legs out, with her knees nearly touching her chin. Afterwards Moll's husband went around pubs, challenging any woman in Saddleworth and Marsden to beat her, offering five crown pies as a prize.

There was also a smoking contest for the old women. Sitting in a row on a raised stand, at the inn, they were each given the same amount of tobacco, and at a given signal, lit up to see who would finish first. They were soon puffing away, hardly visible in a cloud of smoke with supporters encouraging them.

Alexandra Park Pagoda

The pagoda was built in 1899 on the site of an earlier observatory, to mark the Borough's 50th year. On the day of the laying of the foundation stone, key buildings in the town were floodlit and there were fireworks. Amongst the features of the meteorological observatory was a base made from Aberdeen granite with a storage area below, and a rain gauge at the top. At the side, a carved panel indicates the building was the responsibility of the Sanitary Committee.

A local journalist described the pagoda as 'ghastly' in 1952 but the parks superintendent thought it 'rather nice' and invited ideas on how to use the old building.

By 1976 the pagoda was roped off and the council considered demolishing it because of its poor condition. One councillor was reported as saying 'I would like to see it fall down, I think it is going to be a great burden on us in the future'. However it was a grade two listed building and could not be demolished. The following year it cost £17,000 to renovate it through a job creation scheme, with most of the money coming from a Government grant.

The first Alexandra Park observatory

OLDHAM LOCAL STUDIES & ARCHIVES

Blind Joe

The statue was erected in 1868 in memory of Joseph Howarth who had been blind from birth. In his childhood he had learned to find his way around the town with the aid of a stick. It was claimed he could get to Manchester unaided.

He was elected as town cryer in 1820 and for over forty years had conscientiously carried out his duties as a bell-man or town cryer, giving out information about local bargains. One of his jobs was to open and close Tommyfield Market where he also had a pie and muffin stall. At 11.30 on a Saturday night it was his duty to ring his bell to bring the market to a close.

Howarth was a man of good character, a Methodist local preacher, with a fine bass voice and a good orator in demand throughout the country. He had an amazing memory and was able to recite chapters from the Bible once they had been read to him. When he was memorizing something he would hold up his left hand to his face with the fingers outstretched and then touch the finger tips with his right hand.

He lodged at the home of Henry and Alice Ramsden at Mill Street, Yorkshire Street and Greaves Street. He retired when his impressive memory began to fail. When he died, he was buried in the Ramsden family grave at Chadderton. Huge crowds came to the unveiling of his statue in Alexandra Park, and after the speeches his bell was rung and the peals could be heard throughout the park.

The Rhyming bellman

Howarth's successor was Thomas Whitworth who was known as the Rhyming Bellman. In contrast to Howarth, who always dressed in a grey coat and top hat, Whitworth was a more colourful character who wore a green coat with brass buttons and a hat with the word 'bellman' in glittering letters. During his early years the announcements were given in rhyme. Later as his health declined, the rhymes stopped and he gave up the job in 1868 when he was unable to stand. His wife deputised for him, also speaking in rhyme. Whitworth died the following year, and although the job was advertised, he was to be the last town cryer of Oldham.

King Dody the Oldham giant

In the 18th century, Joseph Scholes, nicknamed 'Dody', was probably the biggest man to have lived in Oldham at 6ft 6ins and weighing 26 stones. He was known as a gentle giant, once overturning a cart to stop troublemakers disrupting an outdoor Methodist meeting.

Although he remained a civilian, he was a recruiting sergeant for the army and later governor of the Oldham workhouse. Afterwards he became a pot-seller. As his weight increased he transferred the business outside his shop premises. He would sit on the ground in the middle of his goods and customers would throw over money to him.

By the time of his death in 1814 at his home in Henshaw Street, his weight had increased to 37 stones. The door jamb had to be removed to get the nine ft-wide coffin out of the house. It took several teams of twelve men to carry the coffin to Oldham parish church, watched by thousands of people who lined the route.

Scholes was buried in the church but was later reburied in the graveyard following building work in 1826. However this was not to be his final resting place because the plot was required for his grandson and his remains were transferred into a coal basket for re-burial. Items of his clothing - a waistcoat and knee breeches - had been preserved as curiosities. His massive coffin is in the crypt of Oldham Church.

Site of a knight's coffin in the crypt

Joe o' Ragstones

Joseph Radcliffe was a recluse who lived in a ramshackle house near Buckstones Road, Denshaw. Although coming from a well-to-do family and educated at a grammar school he chose to live in a run-down property nicknamed locally as 'Ragstones', with most of the windows boarded up. He visited Paris and became a supporter of Napoleon and the French Republic and on his return he always greeted people with 'Napoleon for ever'.

He was undoubtedly wealthy but acted strangely with his finances. After returning from France he remembered he owed 6d and went straight back to settle the small debt. He owed 10d to a man in New York and went to the enormous expense of travelling back over the Atlantic. When he found that treacle was a halfpenny cheaper in Rochdale than in Denshaw he made the longer journey. He died aged 75 on a bed of dried grass, surrounded by loose stones.

Oldham tradesmen
Carvings on a row of shops
at Henshaw Street

Rag pudding

It is reputed to have originated in Oldham where there would have been plentiful supplies of scrap cloth from the local cotton mills. It was known by many as 'meat pie' and consisted of minced meat and onions with suet pastry. The ingredients were wrapped in cloth, fastened with safety pins and then boiled for about three hours. It would have been a cheap meal consumed by many workers when they came home at 'dinner-time'. Once used, the cloth was washed and even ironed. At 'tea-time' the meal would have been just jam and bread. Rag pudding was popular around the northern mill towns and is still enjoyed today with slight variations.

Flood markers

A storm on 11 July 1872 across the region caused severe damage. Bridges, mill dams, and mill machinery were destroyed. In Delph (left), two streams met and the water rushed into the village. At Uppermill (top), Thomas Rhodes, an employee at the Victoria Mills, drowned after trying to cross the river while intoxicated. When the waters subsided, haystacks were seen on the tops of trees.

Billy Butterworth - the Glodwick hermit

Butterworth dressed in the style of King Charles with a silk jacket, a black cap with ostrich feather, and a long black beard down to his waist. He was popular not only with local people but was also a friend of the gentry.

He built himself a stone cottage at Glodwick Lows, made from stones, earth and moss. Inside there was a chapel and an observatory with a camera obscura with a range of up to five miles. Outside he had a kitchen garden and an area of grottos, seating and statues. From his terrace he had a commanding view of the district and would use either a bell or megaphone to call for provisions. He reputedly earned around five guineas a day from sales of ginger beer, cakes and biscuits.

He was a professional actor, sang and gave recitations at public houses, and organised pantomimes, with his Bluebeard character, a favourite with Oldhamers. In one of his productions, he and four miners playing both ends of an elephant caused confusion when they fell through the stage. He was badly shaken by a fire which destroyed his home known as 'Elysian Cot'. Although he tried to rebuild it he died soon after, aged 52.

Standedge tunnel

This is the southern entrance to the Standedge tunnel between Diggle and Marsden - the longest, and deepest in the country. It is three and a quarter miles long and 636 ft down at the deepest point. It took sixteen years to build with the use of gunpowder, picks and shovels. The tunnel is on the twenty mile long Huddersfield Narrow Canal which runs between Ashton-under-Lyne and Huddersfield.

Benjamin Outram, the engineer, died before the canal was finished and the project was completed on an advisory basis by the great engineer Thomas Telford. It opened for canal traffic in 1811 and became a busy commercial waterway. Weaving mill settlements sprung up in the vicinity of the canal at Greenfield, Mossley and Stalybridge producing woollen fabric for transportation. Each day around thirty boats set off from the wharf at Dobcross.

The narrow boats were horse-drawn but as there was no towpath in the tunnel, the boats had to be 'legged' through by men lying on the boat and using their legs along the walls or roof of the tunnel. The horse that had been pulling the boat was taken over the hill to the far canal entrance. Road vehicles eventually became the preferred way of transporting the goods and canal traffic became limited to delivering coal. The last working boat to use the tunnel passed through in 1921 and by 1944 the canal was officially abandoned.

In 1971 the Huddersfield Canal Society, in partnership with the local authorities and British Waterways, set out proposals to restore the canal. This was a massive undertaking because parts of the route had been filled in, locks were derelict and bridges had been removed or culverted. Work began in 1981 and the canal reopened twenty years later, at a cost of £45m.

The tunnel entrance and car park is off Station Road Diggle.

Longdendale Miniature Castle

Also known as Matley Castle, it was originally a cottage until it was converted in the 1880s. Known as 'New Bent Farm' since about 1791, it had been occupied not only by farmers but also a felt-hat maker. William Whitworth, the owner of a baby linen business in Manchester bought the property and re-styled it into the present-day castle and farm house.

The property has attracted a number of interesting occupants - Dacres Olivier, a relation of actor Sir Laurence Olivier lived there until 1896, Edwin Strong, director of a Hyde engineering company owned it for almost ten years and in the 1970s it was the home of Derek Brandon, a producer who pioneered the production of American football on British TV. The farm is currently in the ownership of the Winn family who have been grazing cattle here since the early 1940s. Running directly beneath the property is the Mottram Water tunnel, completed in 1850 to bring water from the Longdendale reservoirs to Manchester, via Godley.

(The property is privately owned and not accessible to the public)

Tunnel ventilation shaft

Cheshire Rifleman Inn

The Old Thirteenth Cheshire Astley Volunteer Rifleman Corps Inn, Astley Street Stalybridge, is the pub with the longest name in Britain. It was known as the New Inn when it opened about 1855, but was renamed The Thirteenth Mounted Cheshire Rifleman Inn when a drill hall was opened nearby. 100,000 men nationally had enrolled for the Volunteers equiping themselves with weapons and uniform, in response to growing threats of war abroad. Many of the locals were to serve with the Cheshire Regiment in the 1899 Boer War, in South Africa.

Over the years, the pub's owners have added three extra words to its title to keep it in first place. In contrast, the 'Q' inn on Market Street is credited with having the shortest pub name in the country.

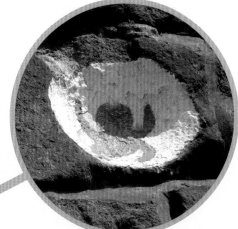

Frog Stone

Set high into the wall of the cutting of Roe Cross Road, it is supposed to be the remains of a frog entombed for millions of years found inside a split stone. However the name is more likely to be derived from the hollowed-out area of a brick which is known as a 'frog'.

Ashton -
the 'New Jerusalem'

The former pub known as the Odd Whim, in Ashton was going to be one of four gatehouses heralding the coming of the 'New Jerusalem' when Christ returns to earth. The buildings would be joined by a wall to form an inner temple area. This was according to prophet John Roe, a member of the Christian Israelites - a breakaway church in the 1820s.

Roe came to Ashton in 1820 believing the town was a 'most favoured' place for believers to live. He was publicly baptised in the River Medlock near Park Bridge in 1823 and the following year circumcised at a meeting. The group believed in living by strict Mosaic laws which included men having beards, no use of false teeth, and administering corporal punishment to those who disobeyed. Members were encouraged to inform on each other if they saw any breach of the law. Roe was described as a 'stern man with a forbidding aspect' and 'dreaded by all who followed him'.

The former Odd Whim pub

Over his life-time he made several false claims including, while preaching in a field at Ashton, 'A light shall break forth from this place which shall enlighten the whole town ...' However he was partly right - it later became the site where gas lights were made.

In 1830 he was charged with alleged immoral conduct with the young women who accompanied him on his missions. Ironically, the trial was held at the Odd Whim. It was a controversial event with fighting and two of the jury having to be replaced. After six days he was acquitted but there was much ill-feeling towards him in the town and he left hurriedly. Many of his followers cut off their beards and left the organisation. He returned two months later but riots convinced him to leave again.

He and his followers went to live in Yorkshire where a huge mansion was built for him, and referred to as the 'Temple'. It was mainly funded by Australian supporters and was said to resemble Melbourne Town Hall. He died in Australia during a tour in 1863, much to the disappointment of his followers who were known as 'beardies'. They demanded their subscriptions back because he had promised them he would never die.

A remnant of Christian Israelites remained in Ashton. They could be recognized by their beards and broad-brimmed hats. Those who were shop-keepers closed from six on Friday to six the following day to observe the Jewish Sabbath.

Hibbert's garden folly

The Gothic style folly is in the garden of a day nursery, on Mottram Road, Godley. It was built around 1850 by Joseph Hibbert who owned the property known as Brook Bank. He was the son of Randal Hibbert, a mill owner and merchant. Joseph was a solicitor and clerk to the local magistrates and interested in local history. His history of Hyde and its neighbourhood was published in 1856. He had seven sons and died in 1860. The folly, once used as a pigsty, has a 1767 datestone which must be from another site.

A LECTURE
UPON
HYDE,
IN THE COUNTY OF CHESTER,
AND ITS NEIGHBOURHOOD:
DELIVERED AT THE
HYDE MECHANICS' INSTITUTION,
ON THE 18TH NOVEMBER, 1856,
BY
MR. JOSEPH HIBBERT.
——
MR. JOHN TAYLOR, CHAIRMAN.
——
SECOND EDITION.
——
HYDE:
PRINTED AND SOLD BY ELIZA WILLIAMSON,
CLARENDON PLACE.

Hartshead Pike

The Pike is on the earlier site of a beacon or signalling station because of its prominence over four counties. In 1750 a local court leet ruled 'If any persons shall in any way abuse Hartshead Pike either with stones or clods or in any way deface the weather mark, they shall for every such offence, lose 3s 4d'. This had possibly not deterred vandals because the tower was in such a bad condition by 1751 that it had to be rebuilt by public conscription. It included the inscription 'Look well at me before you go, And see you nothing at me throw'.

A man was killed by lightning here in July 1776, although miraculously the child he was holding in his arms and his wife and another child next to him escaped without injury. A 1794 lightning storm caused a huge crack in the structure and after years of neglect it fell down in 1820. The circular ruins can still be seen today.

Hartshead Pike was the site for Methodist preacher Joseph Raynor's fiery sermons in the 1830s. During one meeting, a strong wind arose which made people think of the violent wind at Pentecost. Raynor's forthright campaigning for the poor made him an enemy with some mill owners and the clergy. He was sent to prison for 18 months for attending 'an unlawful meeting', but he continued to fight for the oppressed from his cell.

The tower was re-erected by public subscription to celebrate the marriage of Edward, Prince of Wales, to Princess Alexandra of Denmark.

A crowd of 3000 in 1863 watched as the foundation stone was laid over a sunken bottle containing newspapers, coins, local poetry and a document of the event. Lord Stamford donated both the land and the materials to build it. The main structure was completed the following year by unemployed cotton workers and the spire was added later after sufficient funds had been raised. On the day of the royal marriage, a beacon was lit on Hartshead which burned through to the next day.

A severe gale in 1927 blew the top off the monument and large pieces of stone rolled down the hillside. The combination of weather and vandalism at the tower led to an appeal for £500 to restore it. The following year the work had been completed due to £400 being subscribed, with a further £50 donated by the 'Lady Bountiful', Dame Sarah Lees of Oldham, in memory of the time when 'there was no tower, only a circle of stones, amongst which I and my sisters had many merry games'.

A caretaker lived there and the public paid to go up the tower. Later pop and sweets were sold there for a ha'penny until the last World War when the entrance was closed off. Nearby was one of the smallest chapels in the region, St Augustine's, established in 1814. It was said to have just ten pews and has been converted into a house.

A beacon was lit here to celebrate the coronation of King Edward VII in 1902. Another was ignited at the Pike on St George's Day 1965 to mark an appeal to save Britain's coastline. It was one of 700 and was visible for miles. In 1981 the tower was cleaned and the windows painted to mark the wedding of Prince Charles and Lady Diana Spencer.

Left top: In the foreground, the remains of the earlier pike.
Left: The tower pre-1864.
Right: The present day pike with its history recorded in stone.

The King of Hyde

Frederick Howard Whittaker lived in a curious building known as 'Whittaker's Whim' at Hunt Croft Quarry, Silverhill. From the road it appeared to be a large two-storey shop, but from the quarry it looked like an old mill. Whittaker sold off the contents of the mill in 1874 and it remained derelict for years.

Wearing a huge hat with ostrich feathers or a yellow cap, he rode around the town on a horse. He was the nick-named 'The King of Hyde', presumably because of the amount of local property he owned.

He had been the manager of his uncle's cotton mill in Hyde for nearly thirty years but when the business collapsed around 1871 he acquired property and shares. Whittaker's behaviour became increasingly odd, possibly through drunkenness. He had been seen around town looking unkempt and with an ink bottle tied around his coat with red ribbon and had smashed the windows of his own pub, the Sportsman. On another occasion he organised a dance behind the Eagle and Oak Inn for gypsies camping nearby.

He had lots of ideas which he left with his solicitor to patent such as a railway across the Atlantic to America suspended by balloons. He was sent to Chester Castle Prison in 1879 for unpaid debts and after-wards left his wife and children to live in Penrith and later Heysham, where he lived until his death in 1884 aged 71 leaving £40,000.

Roe Cross stone

A whitened boulder in a garden on Old Road, Roe Cross, has connec-tions to the legend of Ralph de Stavelegh who fought in the Crusades. When he did not return, another knight who wanted his widow's lands and possessions asked her to marry him. At the wedding ceremony, a mysterious stranger appeared who kept his face hidden under a cape. He dramatically revealed his identity and the knight fled. The 'stranger' was Ralph who had managed to escape from prison and travel back across Europe and so he and his wife were re-united.

Old Jud's cellar house

Jud, whose real name was George Hurley, is said to have lived in a cellar dwelling below a row of houses known as 'The Grandstand' in Broadbottom. He was a 'pig stricker' - slaughterman, possibly even carrying out his work here. Local children were afraid of him and kept their distance because he always carried a large slaughterman's knife around the village. George was more interested in how to earn enough to buy a drink and he died alone in his cellar house.

Robin Hood's Picking Rods

This is reputed to be where the famous outlaw strung his bow around the stones. Another story suggests that women and land were sold here. This type of monument, sometimes without the shafts, is to be seen in a number of places in the region and known by different names.

There is a similar stone at Bowstones near Lyme Park, and bases without shafts known as 'the plague stone' near Disley and at Stretford. Other bases are to be found in Disley churchyard and possibly at Abbot's Chair near Charlesworth. The shafts would have supported cross heads and thought to date from the 9th or 10th century. They were broken up in the 16th century and buried, then later used as boundary markers or guide posts. They are not necessarily in their original locations; for example, the 'Robin Hood era' had long gone when the 'Picking Rods' were put in their present location near Chisworth.

The 'Stalybridge Infant'

Sam Hurst, born in Marsden, was the national bare-knuckle champion 1860-61. He came to Stalybridge in 1857 and by then was six feet two and half inches and weighed 14st 12lb. He worked in the local ironworks foundry and could put a fist through a door panel and carry a kitchen dresser under one arm. Working as a 'bouncer' at the White House pub, he would carry out trouble-makers with one hand and drop them in the middle of the street. The owner of the White House saw the potential in Sam and arranged a wrestling match against Daniel Heywood at the Copenhagen Grounds, Newton Heath in September 1858 for £100.

Nicknamed 'the infant' as a joke because of his huge physique, Hurst fought Tom Paddock at Aldermaston on 6 November 1860 to become the English bare knuckle-champion for a prize of £400 (the equivalent of £34,000 today). Hurst was not a skillful fighter and relied mainly on his strength. The fight lasted five rounds with Hurst pressing forward. Paddock was felled by a strong blow which broke three of his ribs.

Hurst next fought Jem Mace, the 'Norfolk Hero', at Medway Island, Kent 18 June 1861. Hurst was not fully fit after falling down some steps and breaking his leg while celebrating his last win with his drunken supporters. The injury caused him to limp for the rest of his life.

At the beginning of the match it seemed like a David and Goliath contest because Hurst was much taller and heavier than Mace. But Hurst was no match for his opponent's superior speed and agility. He was badly beaten around the head and after six rounds the crowd were calling for the fight to be stopped. Hurst gamely continued until Mace almost reluctantly hit him with one last heavy blow and a sponge was thrown in to signal the end of the fight. The sound of the punches was likened to that of hitting raw meat.

TAMESIDE LOCAL STUDIES & ARCHIVES

Sam Hurst

Mace went on to become one of the sport's most colourful and notable fighters. He continued to fight into his 60's and gave exhibitions until he was 79. Jem was so worried about Hurst's condition that he sat by his bedside for several days until he had sufficiently recovered. Sam Hurst never fought again and there was great disappointment in Stalybridge - many had bet their savings on him. When they saw Hurst in the street afterwards they turned their backs on him.

The following month he married the daughter of a Manchester publican. In 1862 he became landlord of the Wilton Arms in Shudehill Manchester and took over the Botanical Gardens beerhouse at Hyde in 1865. The following year he became landlord of the Glass House tavern on Oldham Road Manchester until 1871.

Over the years he was fined for his involvement in a number of drunken brawls and betting offences. He took part in exhibition matches around the country, including one with his old adversary Jem Mace, while his wife managed the beerhouse and looked after their five young children. His heavy drinking and long absences led her to take the children and move to Oldham. By 1881 Hurst was listed as a shoe-maker and living in Manchester. He suffered from bronchitis and Stalybridge's national champion died in poverty the following year aged 53.

Sam Hurst

Escape from death

Built into the wall at Mossley Parish Church, a memorial shows a girl of 18 in a shroud raising the lid of her coffin. Catherine Kenworthy, the only child of Cornelius and Dorothy, was said to have had an outstanding intellect and to have been well-loved in the community.

The memorial, which had been moved from the earlier church building, symbolises the Christian belief of the dead rising at the return of Jesus. Some people twisted its meaning by suggesting that the girl was in a trance when she was buried in 1776 and is seen escaping from the coffin.

The rather frightening feature was used as a punishment, with misbehaving children being made to stand next to it.

The 'ghost train'

Also known as the 'Parliamentary' train, it is an odd one-way rail service between Stalybridge and Stockport which operates just one run each Friday. There used to be an hourly service both ways on this short stretch of line but because of a reworking of the the trans-Pennine service, has become redundant. However, in order to avoid costly and time-consuming Parliamentary procedures of officially closing the line, the railway company has to provide a minimal service. The line is also used for freight and occasional diverted passenger trains. This unusual service, along the buffet at Stalybridge Station which still retains its Victorian fittings and serves the real ale and refreshments including black peas, makes for an interesting trip out.

Ashton Moss celery

Work began in 1832 to reclaim around 200 acres of peat bog to the west of the town. The peat was between five and six feet thick, and below was a layer of well-preserved prehistoric oak tree trunks. Before the 1830s, the Moss had been described as a 'shaking bog' and virtually impassable. The Earl of Stamford funded the work which involved laying a foundation of clay, gravel and sand.

It would probably have been made into meadow land but its growing qualities were soon utilised and by 1834 Swedish turnips from the Moss were exhibited at the annual meeting of the Manchester Agricultural Society to great acclaim.

Eventually the Moss was a patchwork of plots belonging to farms and market gardeners, but with few trees, hedges or fences.

The herbs, fruit, vegetables, and in particular, the 'early' celery grown here in July, became world famous. It is claimed that the ground was partly fertilised by the dung of tigers and elephants brought from Belle Vue in Manchester.

The farmers and market gardeners took their produce to Manchester but also sold it at Ashton Market and around the streets.

One of the most famous market gardeners on the Moss was Bill Sowerbutts who became a regular panellist on the Gardeners' Question Time radio programme. The Moss was also previously noted for the rare ferns growing there. It is hoped, locally, that 70 allotment plots on the Moss will be opened for cultivation.

The Black Knight

For many years there was a pageant featuring the legendary knight at Ashton. The origins of the Black Knight are unclear, but the custom also known as 'Riding the Black Lad' took place on Easter Monday. Originally, an effigy made of straw and covered in paper was paraded on a horse through the town and then hung in the market place before being destroyed by bullets, arrows and beating.

The figure was based on the legend of the unpopular Sir Ralph de Assheton in the 15th century. He was said to have tyrannised the area as he rode around on a big black horse. The manor had been infested with a yellow weed, corn marigold, and anyone found guilty of not removing it was punished. If they resisted, they were rolled down a hill in a barrel spiked with nails. Others were dispatched by hanging at Gallows Fields. Assheton finally got his comeuppance when he was shot during one of his visits. Therefore the parade was popular because it was a good day out celebrating a rebellion against oppression and authority.

It seems likely that the custom was linked to a much earlier practice of celebrating the end of winter with a character known as the 'Blake Lad'. The Court Leet accounts of 1758 contain the first reference to the 'usual five shillings' given to the making of the black lad effigy.

Over the years the ceremony, which attracted crowds of over 100,000, became more elaborate with the inclusion of a person dressed in armour on a black horse and an Arab chieftain known as Osman Digna, who travelled in a gig. The occasion attracted much drunkenness and rowdiness, and increasing numbers of knights and effigies appeared in the parade.

The pageants continued periodically until 1954 when it became too difficult to organise. The knight was once more paraded through the town as part of the celebrations to open the Arcades shopping centre in 1995 and the event went on until 2005. The knight appeared in later local festivals and then the parade reappeared in 2007, but there have been none since. Over the years, this unique pageant of horse-drawn carriages, floats and people in costume had been a great favourite with many people. Marjan Wouda won the commission to design a Black Knight bronze sculpture for the Arcades Shopping Centre in 1995 and it is now on view, re-coloured in black, at the Council offices.

Fire death memorial

Two children died in an isolated hut about a mile outside Tintwistle. They had been left alone in bed asleep when the house caught fire. Their father, James Forshaw, was a sub-contractor on the Arndale Reservoir and had left for work at 4am. They were one of the many navvy families who lived in small shanty towns along the valley. The mother had gone outside to weed the potato patch when the tragedy occurred. At the inquest it was admitted that the bed had been just a yard away from the fireplace and the jury returned a verdict of accidental death due to gross neglect. The house was made of rough stones and clay and roofed with straw thatch and may have had a potato sack as a door. The Marker Stone is built into a stone wall on the reservoir side of the road, close to a lay-by on the A628.

Tithe Stone

The stone originates from the times when farmers paid a tithe or tax to the parish. At this point, twice a year, produce was handed over and then taken away for storage in nearby tithe barns. The stone, also known as the 'Twarl Stone' is in the Twarl Hill or Twirl Hill district within the parish of Ashton. Tithes continued to be paid until 1831 and the words were carved on the stone around 1840.

It may also have been used as a plague stone. During times of the disease outbreak, traders would place their money on the stone and then stand back to avoid contagion. Other traders would then leave goods at the spot here at Twirl Hill Road.

Winter's jewellers

The mechanical figures at the clockhouse, known as the 'three jacks' - a guardsman, a sailor and Old Father Tyme were carved from an old fighting ship's oak beam. They strike the bells every fifteen minutes and have become one of Stockport's most famous sights. It was said to keep the best time of any clock in the town.

Jacob Winter

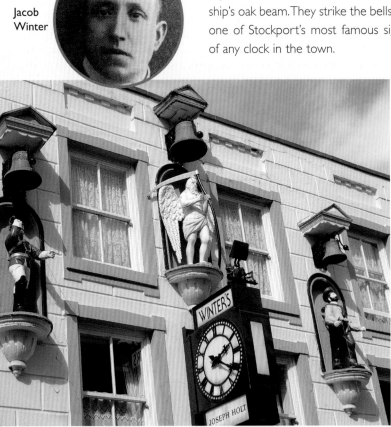

Both Hillgate and Underbank have been noted centres for clock and watchmaking since the early 1700s.

Born in 1865 in London, Jacob Winter was the son of a Polish master tailor. By 1877, the family had moved to Manchester and at the age of 15, Jacob was apprenticed to jeweller, WT Glover at Mealhouse Brow. In 1887 he opened his own business in Lower Hillgate, Stockport. Passers-by could see him at work in the front window.

He moved to the shop which became known as the Clock House in 1890. By 1896 he also had a business at Alderley Edge.

The 1901 Census indicated he was living at Heaton Road. In 1903, as well as acquiring the shop next door and extending at the back, alterations were made to the frontage of Winter's so that part of the window display could be lowered each evening into the basement by means of hydraulics.

As well as his jewellery business, he also owned hotels in Blackpool and Colwyn Bay and held the licences of several cinemas. He was prominent in the local life of the town, being a councillor serving on council committees, a magistrate, and a member of other organizations. He was regarded as a leader and a role model in the Jewish community.

Jacob Winter died in 1935, aged 70, at Colwyn Bay leaving substantial donations to local charities. The business remained in the Winter family until 1980 and the property on Little Underbank, is now a pub - aptly named 'Winters'.

The clock mechanism

The stone on Ewrin Lane near the junction with Hooleyhey Lane

Turner memorial, Rainow

This records the death of John Turner during a snow storm in 1735. The original stone was made by James Mellor from the nearby gardens but this has been replaced by a memorial with an incorrect date. Turner was a pack-horse man and had been trying to make his way home on Christmas Eve during a severe snowstorm. The bodies of Turner and his horses were found the following day along with the mysterious print of a woman's shoe at the scene. The bells from the packhorses were acquired by Mellor, except the one from the leading horse which was used as a meal bell at a nearby farm.

Woodbank garden folly

George Emmott, a retired civil engineer and former first manager of Oldham Corporation gas and water-works, lived at Woodbank in Disley from 1867 and is thought to have built the tower as an observatory. He used the second floor as a study where there was a table and a couch. He was a consulting engineer on projects in Britain and on the continent and later, a manufacturer in the cotton industry. Emmott was also founder of New Mills gas works.

He was a Quaker and had a reputation for integrity and fairness in his dealings. Later, when he was badly affected by rheumatism, his coachman and valet, John Fox, used to carry him up the tower so that he could continue to enjoy the views.

There would have been impressive views of Lyme Cage and across Cheshire and Wales from here. Emmott died at Woodbank aged 92 in 1890 but his unmarried daughter, Elizabeth, continued to live there until her death six years later.

The land for Woodbank was purchased by Leigh Slater in 1847 from Thomas Legh. Slater, born in Pendlebury, owned the Grove cotton spinning mill in Disley, by the River Goyt and died at Southport in 1861.

Amongst the later owners of Woodbank, there have been textile merchants, a retired dentist who developed improvements in false teeth and Dr Bertram Prentice - Principal of Salford Technical College in the 1930s.

(The tower is on private property and not open to the public.)

Female 'Bachelor' grave

In St Peter's Church graveyard, Prestbury, there is a memorial to a female bachelor. It reads 'Here lyeth ..the body of ... Sarah Pickford...who was interred August 17, 1705, and died a bachelour in the 48 year of her age'. It is believed there is also a reference in Shakespeare to unmarried women being known as bachelors before they were referred to as spinsters. Also buried here, in 1752, is Paul Mason who was the father and grandfather of 94 children.

Chinese dovecote

Otherwise known as 'The Pigeon Cote' it is on the mill pond, off Station Road, belonging to the former Strines calico print works which was established in 1792. Corn for the birds was sent out on a raft or a flat wooden box tied to rope.

Clayton's tower

Clayton's Tower, Bollington, a castellated round chimney shaft with arrowslits, was built in 1840 for William Clayton. It is seen from Windmill Lane and was constructed in readiness for working coal seams, but Clayton died soon afterwards and it was never used for its intended purpose.

Secrets of Abney Hall

The grounds of Abney Hall Cheadle contain an artificial waterfall in the gardens and a ventilation shaft known as the 'Owl Tower'. The ornamental shaft with a weather vane drew air into the extensive cellars to ventilate the surplus fruit stored there from the gardens. Warm air from a basement furnace was blown onto the walled vegetable garden through openings. The tower was so named because it was designed to be a place for birds to live.

Owl tower

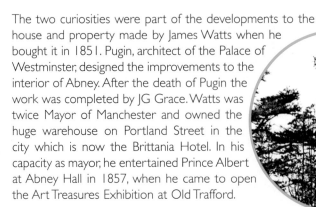

The two curiosities were part of the developments to the house and property made by James Watts when he bought it in 1851. Pugin, architect of the Palace of Westminster, designed the improvements to the interior of Abney. After the death of Pugin the work was completed by JG Grace. Watts was twice Mayor of Manchester and owned the huge warehouse on Portland Street in the city which is now the Brittania Hotel. In his capacity as mayor, he entertained Prince Albert at Abney Hall in 1857, when he came to open the Art Treasures Exhibition at Old Trafford.

Agatha Christie, a relation of the Watts, stayed at the Hall on many occasions and is said to have found the place inspirational. 'After the Funeral' was set at Abney and aspects of the house and grounds are found in seven of her works. In the foreword to 'The Adventure of the Christmas Pudding' she wrote glowingly about Christmases she spent there and of the kindness and hospitality she had received.

Above: Family pets graves
Below: The artificial waterfall

Following her sensational disappearance in December 1926, she came to Abney Hall. She was reported missing and then her overturned car was found by an embankment. A big police search was unsuccessful but she was later recognised as a guest registered as 'Teresa Neeles from Capetown' staying at a spa hotel in Harrogate and was brought back to Cheadle by her husband. It was said at the time that she had suffered a breakdown with a loss of memory. However it seems her mysterious absence was more likely related to her husband's recent request for a divorce. It is believed she staged her dramatic disappearance to provoke a response from him.

Abney remained in the Watts family until it was sold in 1958 and its contents auctioned. Amongst the lots was a coach and a four-poster bed used by the Prince Consort during his Manchester visit, a pair of Queen Victoria's silk stockings, Oliver Cromwell's baby clothes, a lock of Napoleon's hair and a nightshirt worn by William IV. It took ten days to sell the 'treasure house' of Watts' belongings, including huge collections of art, pottery, old fire-arms and furniture.

Abney was originally known as 'The Grove', after the print works of that name on the site and had been built in 1847 as a wedding present for Alfred Orrell, a former mayor of Stockport, but he died the same year aged just 33. He is said to have hidden two thousand golden guineas somewhere in the hall. A steam locomotive based at Paddington was named after the hall in 1940. The nameplate, after its withdrawal from service in 1964, was displayed in the main entrance of the hall.

The local urban district council purchased Abney in 1958 to become Cheadle Town Hall. In addition to council meetings, it also became the venue for a weekly magistrates' court. Following local government reorganisation in 1974, furniture from the hall was removed to Bramall Hall and Lyme Hall, and a large part of the grounds were sold off.

White Nancy

The site at Bollington had been a centuries-old warning beacon of invasion, and would have been known as a military or 'ordnance' beacon. Therefore 'Nancy' is probably derived from 'ordnance' and refers not only to the beacon but also the hill. In 1810 the beacon was described as a 'small rotunda of brick'. An 1816 newspaper report refers to the hill and the beacon as 'the Northern Nancy'.

It is believed the present folly was built the following year by the Gaskell family, who lived at North End Farm and Ingersley Hall, to commemorate the 1815 victory at Waterloo.

Later maps show it was in use as a summerhouse with a black iron-studded door, window, stone table and stone benches around the wall. Also, from Ingersley Hall it would have made a good eye-catcher on the skyline. The assumption that 'Nancy' referred to a member of Gaskell family, or was the name of the lead horse dragging up the slab for the table, would seem to be unfounded.

The folly has always been white, except during the last World War when it was painted green, black and khaki to blend in with the landscape to confuse enemy pilots. However, it has sometimes been secretly painted to look like a Christmas pudding, Father Christmas, Easter egg or Union Jack.

After vandalism of the structure, including the removal of the stone ball on the top, the entrance was sealed around 1935. A new ball was added, and 'Nancy' was plastered over. There has been a tradition of celebration bonfires here since the 1863 marriage of the Prince of Wales.

In 1989 it became the subject of an April Fool joke when there was an application to turn it into a single-person dwelling. The local town council featured Nancy on stamps issued in 2003.

Lyme Cage

The first building on this site at Lyme Park was erected about 1520. By 1737 it had been completely rebuilt. It was known as 'The Cage' and may have been used to temporarily hold local criminals in the late 19th century. It is thought the name came from its similarity to an ornamental birdcage. The Cage was used as a vantage point to watch the hunt and as a banqueting hall. Deer hunting continued at Lyme until the late 18th century when shooting became popular.

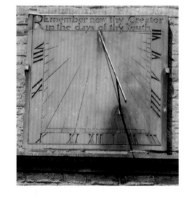

In order to win a 500 guinea bet for his master, Squire Legh, Joseph Watson, keeper of the deer at Lyme, in the 18th century famously drove 40 deer down to Windsor Great Park. He continued to hunt until he was 96 and was said to have consumed a gallon of beer a day until he died age aged 104!

Park staff were housed at The Cage from the mid 1800s until the 1920s. The last occupant, Mr Howard, used to allow visitors in for a penny, in 1929. During the last World War it was used as a lookout by the Home Guard.

The high doorways in the ground floor enabled horses to be ridden into the building. The main reception room is above, with the service room at the top. All the floors are linked by a spiral stone staircase. The Cage was officially opened in 1999 to the public, after restoration costing £545,000.

Left: The first floor room where the hunt banquets took place. There was no water supply so it would have been brought from the Hall.

Inset: A strange bottle mark on the fireplace.

Below: The large doors for the horse riders.

Lyme lantern folly tower

The tower was formerly the top of the 16th century house at Lyme Hall
before being re-erected here by Lewis Wyatt in the late 18th century.

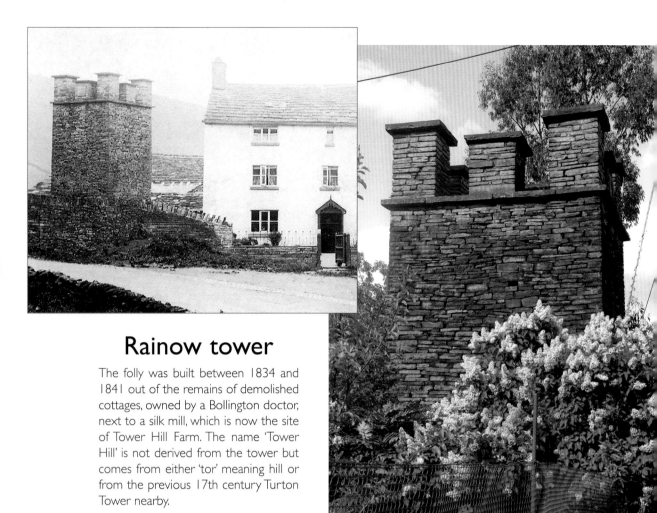

Rainow tower

The folly was built between 1834 and 1841 out of the remains of demolished cottages, owned by a Bollington doctor, next to a silk mill, which is now the site of Tower Hill Farm. The name 'Tower Hill' is not derived from the tower but comes from either 'tor' meaning hill or from the previous 17th century Turton Tower nearby.

Murder stone

William Wood, a weaver, was robbed of £100 and brutally murdered by three men on the Disley to Whaley Bridge road at Disley Tops. He had been on his way home from the Manchester Market to Eyam. Of the two assailants later arrested, one hanged himself at New Bailey Prison, Manchester, before his trial, and the other was hanged at Chester Gaol and his body used for dissection by surgeons. The third man involved was never brought to justice. The memorial was put up in 1874.

Mellor's Gardens

James Mellor began work on the gardens at the rear of his house in the 1840s. They were designed to represent the Pilgrim's Progress story, after being influenced by Swedenborg Church doctrines which fundamentally differed from his original Methodist beliefs. The gardens, which Mellor called 'Garden of correspondence relating to things of this world and Scriptural History' were possibly inspired by the follies and walks at Hawkstone Park Shropshire, and they became a popular attraction for visitors. By 1870 the main layout of the gardens was completed but Mellor continued to add smaller items such as scientific instruments, religious texts and his own sayings inscribed on stones, until he was 90.

The public were allowed in the gardens at any time, and James never tired of explaining the meaning of their elements. A stream runs through the property and he used it to create a pond and weir. There was a summer house 'Bethel' and the stream became 'The River Jordan' and the pond 'The Pool of Siloam'.

A summer house known as the 'The Howling House' had an Aeolian harp in the rear wall. When the doors were opened the wind blew through and caused a strange howling sound from the

The 'Howling House' and the sliding panel where the wind blew onto the harp strings.

harp strings, said to resemble the sounds of souls in torment. Mellor used to throw sulphur into the fire in a dramatic illustration of the burning pits of hell.

He built a chapel in a corner of the garden with a family burial ground. He designed his own four-sided gravestone with an inscription and a space for the date of his death. He was a bachelor and a vegetarian for the last thirty years of his life, and conducted services at the chapel or in his house. His father owned the nearby Hough Hole cotton mill which James later took over, before retiring in the 1850s to pursue his other interest in the gardens.

James Mellor died in 1891 and the property was lived in by members of the Mellor family until it was sold in 1927. Later owners have restored the overgrown garden.

The gardens at Rainow are open the last May Bank Holiday Monday and August Bank Holiday Monday. Guided tours at other times by prior arrangement, ring 01625 573251.

Road-side grave

The grave next to the backs of houses on Didsbury road is a real curiosity. Normally people are buried in consecrated ground but Isaac Thorniley and his wife Hannah's final resting place is in this unusual spot away from a churchyard. The gravestone records that Isaac 'was here interred agreeably to his own request' in 1804 aged 86. Isaac rented a pew at St James Church Didsbury but it is thought that his wife's Unitarian beliefs may be behind the request to be buried elsewhere. The other stone with 'ITH' initials and the date suggest that this was the datestone on their house nearby.

Bramhall folly garden

This demonstrates that folly gardens are not a thing of the past. Phil, the householder, began working on the project around ten years ago. It caused controversy among some neighbours and there were questions of requiring planning permission. The issue was featured on TV and in the newspapers. Thankfully, the work was allowed to continue and with plants added it now effectively blends into leafy Bramhall in a road off Ack Lane.

The good news is that the second part of the garden scheme is now under way with more towers, and gothic features. It will probably take another year to complete and will add something different to the neighbourhood.

Top: the first phase
Below: the latest work

Rat House

T'ing House a square brick summmer House overlooking the river Dean is based on the architecture of the medieval hall and designed in the Chinese style.

Temple of Diana

Adlington Hall garden follies

The 18th century Wilderness Garden was designed by Charles Legh and his wife Hester between 1742 and 1757. It was an informal garden in natural woodland, described in 1890 as 'the most magnificent in the country'.

The estate has been owned by the Legh family since the 14th century. Charles was a cultured man interested in the arts. He wrote the words to a hunting song set to music by Handel who visited Adlington Hall three times. The 'Wilderness Garden' was designed so that from several vantage points the follies could be seen.

The Hermitage ruins possibly had a hired hermit.

The rockwork cascade used to have a statue of Father Tiber on the top but this has been removed to the Water Garden by the Hall.

Brick castle folly c1760 in the former deer park.

Chinese Bridge which has the base of an octagonal summerhouse.

Rat House, a brick building without a roof, destroyed by a fallen tree

Shell Cottage, the first ornamental building in the 'Wilderness' with internal walls covered in shells, pebbles and bands of coloured mirrors - currently under restoration. There is a difference in architectural styles between the formal front and rear of the building with a large rockery. Over the entrance there is the emblem of an urn with the initials of Charles and Hester.

KNUTSFORD
ENGLAND

JOHN O' GROATS
555 MILES

LANDS END
375 MILES

TRAFFORD

Knutsford sanding

While other places used coloured sand to brighten the streets on special occasions, it seems that Knutsford took the process a stage further. The sprinkling of red and white sand floral decorations and verses at weddings is thought only to be found at Knutsford. Sanding also took place on royal occasions such as the Coronation of King George IV and the visit of the Prince and Princess of Wales in 1887. It was used during protests against the Act in 1829 which allowed Catholics to vote, with the slogans 'No popery' and 'Down with Catholics' sanded on the streets. Sanding is perhaps best known during the May Day celebrations when the home of the May Queen and various parts of the town are decorated. The work is done early in the morning by a team of sandmen and their creations have to survive both the weather and passing traffic and feet.

Timperley Early

This is a nationally known rhubarb grown in the Timperley district. The earliest reference to it was in 1920 when Thomas Baldwin, a market gardener at 'Wilford' on Heyes Lane, Timperley, noticed it amongst other varieties of rhubarb. He then propagated it and gave it away to friends. He grew up on his father's farm on Derbyshire Road, Sale and died in 1961. 'Timperly Early' is an offspring of Linnaeaus Rhubarb and is noted not only for the time of year it is grown but also for its flavour, comparative sweetness and its hardiness. Both Herbert Marsland and Harold Warburton, local market gardeners in Timperley claimed to have discovered it, but they seemed to have begun growing it in the 1930s. The Royal Horticultural Society first trialled it in 1949.

Lady Combermere's hooves

The Swan Hotel, Bucklow Hill near Knutsford, has on display the silver-plated hooves of the trotting horse, 'Lady Combermere'. The horse achieved fame after achieving a record-breaking twenty miles in just under an hour. The event took place at the Manchester race course at New Barns close to the present Lowry Centre in Salford in June 1911. In front of a big crowd, the mare made good progress for the first fifteen miles but then began to tire and just managed to complete the distance with a few seconds to spare. The horse was also the record holder in the four mile race in 1895 and also the three miles.

'Lady Combermere' was later sold by Edward Seddon of Sale to Thomas Ackerley, manager of the Swan Inn. When she died thirteen years later, she was buried in the hotel grounds.

The Swan is thought to date back to the fourteenth century, and was stayed in by Bonnie Prince Charlie, as described in the 'Manchester Rebels' by William Hainsworth. The old inn was on the old 'Tally Ho' coach route between Manchester and Chester and was a collecting point for Cheshire cheese being sent to London. The hostelry became popular with the increasing number of motorists coming out to visit Cheshire in the early 1900s.

Above: Thomas Ackerley next to the horse's grave.
Below top: Today the gravestone has been flattened.
Below: Ackerley and Lady Combermere

THE SWAN HOTEL

Sotirios Hazzopulo

Montebellow Castle

This unusual building, slightly hidden by trees, is often missed by those travelling along the busy Chester Road near Bucklow Hill. It was the home of Sotirios Hazzopulo, the former Counsul to Greece and Persia in Manchester. He had the castellated property built on the site around 1889.

Born in Constantinople of Greek parents, he came to Manchester at the age of twenty to join his brother in the family yarn and textiles export business which had been founded in 1858 by his father. When his brother retired, he became the head of the company which was then situated on Oxford Street, Manchester.

He was a popular and prominent member of the Manchester Greek community and served as a Conservative councillor in Salford for three years until 1884. The following year he was appointed as the Greek Consul.

As part of his duties, he entertained the Crown Prince of Greece at his previous home 'Bella Vista' in Broughton, when the Prince visited Manchester in 1887 to see the Royal Jubilee exhibition at Old Trafford. Hazzopulo also attended the Shah of Persia when he came to the City to see the Manchester Ship Canal under construction.

Amongst the many honours conferred upon him were 'The Order of Knight of the Golden Cross' by the King of Greece in appreciation of his visit to Manchester, 'The Golden Cross of Jerusalem' in recognition for raising funds in aid of an earthquake in Greece in 1893; and the war against Turkey in 1897. He was a close friend of King Ferdinand of Bulgaria, and a regular visitor of the great statesman, Mr Gladstone, at his home in Hawarden, Flintshire.

The site at Bucklow Hill, then known as Denfield House, a former boarding school for boys and girls had been purchased by Sotirios Hazzopulo in 1888 for £850. He spent £20,000 on the new property which comprised the house, conservatory, stables, carriage house, hay shed and two other houses. The round tower on the main house had a figure of a man in armour with an outstretched arm. He was listed as living at Montebellow Castle in 1896 after selling 'Bella Vista'.

Both the unusual exterior and interior of Montebellow Castle stirred great local interest. It had its own electricity source, long before that form of power was in general use. It was described by one visitor as 'a rich storehouse of art and other treasures, and brilliant colour quite in accord with European taste and colour'. Its unusual decor led some to suggest mischievously that it was used as a harem, which seems to be a slur on Mr Hazzopulo's good character. He was known for his generosity in entertaining guests and made great efforts to make them feel welcome. For example when a group including a naval officer came to the villa, Sotirius had arranged a display of flags over the lake which signalled 'welcome' to his guests.

Although he had been naturalised in 1873, he continued to observe the customs of his native country. In March 1915 it was announced that the new year of the Persians 1333 would be marked with the raising of the Persian standard at his residence.

After a two-week illness, he died at the castle in April 1916 at the age of around 74. At the burial at Rostherne Church, in the absence of any relatives in this country, his three servants were the 'chief mourners'. These included Miss Mabel Seath who had been his housekeeper for the past eighteen years. His wife, Leonato, had died overseas before 1901, and his married daughters, Catherine and Angelique, were living in France and Corfu. Also attending the funeral were an array of consuls from around Europe. Later in the year, Montebellow Castle and its contents were put up for sale. The property was sold to Lord Egerton for £2,350. The rear of the property has been substantially altered, although the frontage still retains its castellated appearance.

In 1899, Hazzopulo was the victim of a theft as he waited on the platform at Oxford Road Station. His diamond-clustered breast pin worth £50 had been stolen but later a man was arrested and charged at the City Police Court. Sotirios also complained in newspaper correspondence columns about the problem of people on public transport being pestered by street children and others to buy newspapers and matches.

Penny-farthing race

The 'Great Race' takes place every ten years in Knutsford, attracting riders from around the world. It is a three-hour endurance test to see who can do the most circuits around Knutsford Moor. The event, begun in 1980, raises money for charity. Penny-farthing bikes were named after the largest and smallest coins in circulation when they were invented in 1871. The latest race in September 2010, which also included riders on hobby horse and boneshaker bicycles, attracted around 5000 spectators. Knutsford has a tea room off King Street which includes a penny-farthing museum and a working model railway.

Tatton Park sheep tower

The tower is thought to have been built on the site of an earlier structure which had a deep dungeon. A tower is marked on this site at the edge of a field and not linked with a wall, on the 1836-51 tithe map. Also known as the 'Sheep-stealer's tower', it was used to keep watch over the sheep on the estate.

The Tatton Park guide suggests that towers such as this in the Victorian era used to house a hermit whose job was to shock people as they wandered around the gardens.

Hulmes Bridge ferry

The ferry, off Daresbury Avenue, was introduced in 1894 after the bridge crossing the Irwell was removed during the construction of the Manchester Ship Canal. This was part of a Parliamentary Act that guaranteed people the right to cross the waterway without charge.

In 1868 a correspondent to a newspaper reported that Hulme's Bridge was in an unsafe condition. The bridge, which was composed of three planks and an iron handrail on one side, had moved from its foundations. There were also lock gates, sometimes referred to as 'Holmes Lock' with a rise of 3ft 9ins, and a weir. The bridge was close to the water and was frequently submerged. A ferry boat took people across because, even then, there was a public right of way.

In 1884 it was proposed that there would be a steam ferry at Hulme's Bridge. The ferries were running by 1894 at the opening of the Manchester Ship Canal but with oar-propelled boats. Passengers went free but the ferryman at Hulme's Ferry was refusing to take bicycles, prams or wheelbarrows. These had to be taken across the old bridge spanning the Irwell.

The ferry was to be open between 7am and 6pm in the winter, and between 6am and 9pm in the summer for farm labourers who used the ferry. The ferryman's house was built in 1895.

In April 1897, clothing was found near the ferry which belonged to a man who had embezzled around £500 from his employers in Portland Street, Manchester. At first it was thought he had

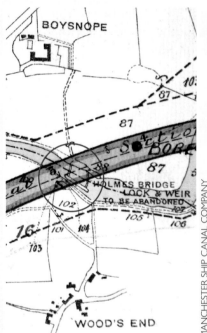

The route of the Ship Canal marked in purple in relation to the meandering River Irwell. The old locks at Hulmes Bridge are ringed.

committed suicide and the canal was dragged, but he was later arrested in Liverpool and charged with the offence.

Shortly before midnight on 16 March 1969, the Manchester Liners' new container ship, 'Manchester Courage' collided with the lower gates at Irlam Lock and ended partly inside the lock. The Canada-bound ship had been launched the previous September and was designed to sail through ice. The collision and the resulting loss of water caused water levels to drop by sixteen feet and the ferry services at Hulme's Bridge and Irlam were suspended. A photograph of the ferry taken just over a week later shows the ferry and backup boat left hanging by ropes after the incident. The canal was closed for eleven days until some vessels were able to pass through a smaller lock, and five weeks before the larger boats could enter the main lock. Fifteen ships were trapped at the Port of Manchester. This was the second major accident at the lock. In 1960 a sand hopper sank here and caused a partial blockage. 'Manchester Courage' went to Middlesbrough for repairs.

Although the early records have been lost, some details are known about the ferrymen. In 1901 the ferryman was Fell Watterson, aged 45, born in the Isle of Man. Edmund Cowlishaw, the ferry master in 1909, was a former rigger born in Birkenhead. His successor in 1911 was Thomas Noall, aged 65, born in St Ives and former master of the vessel 'Uncle Ned' in Plymouth in 1891 who also served on the schooner 'Village Belle' in South Shields in 1901.

Roy Sharratt

By February 1973, the ferry was run by Roy Sharratt who had been there since May 1939, along with Gordon Edwards of Lymm and relief-man George Yates from Irlam. The men worked a five-day week on shifts between 5.30am - 2pm and 2pm-11pm on the rowing boat which carried nine passengers. They made around sixty crossings per shift, taking around 120 people in a day. Roy began as a telephone boy on the Barton Swing Bridge. During his time as ferryman he fell into the heavily polluted Canal twice and also helped to recover two bodies. He and his family lived at the ferryman's cottage for thirty years.

In 1981 there were fears that the service would be closed following the loss of 300 jobs at the Manchester Ship Canal Company. However the company reminded the public that the ferry was protected by an Act of Parliament and that the redundancies reflected the rundown of cargo business to Canada, India and East Africa.

John McDermott was the ferryman here for many years. Once while helping a lady out of the boat during low water with one foot in the boat and the other on the landing stage, his keys fell out of his pocket into the canal. But being an experienced boatman, he had attached his keys to a piece of cork and they remained on the surface and he was able to retrieve them. When McDermott died in 2009, the service was temporarily suspended and re-opened in 2011 with a more limited service. At weekends, a 42ft long barge BML2 is used. It has been re-engined and was built over forty years ago and used to transport lock-gates for British Waterways.

On the opposite bank is the site of the former Boysnope Wharf re-opened by Manchester Corporation Cleansing Department in 1898 on a section of the original route of the River Irwell.

John McDermott taking the author's family across in 1982.

Barges brought night soil here from the Water Street Depot in Manchester to be offloaded onto a thirteen mile narrow gauge (2ft 6in) railway nicknamed 'the muck line' which took it to the tenant farms on Chat Moss. The 2472 acres of bog, 17ft deep in places, was purchased from Sir Humphrey de Trafford. It is thought to be named after St Chad (or Chatley), Bishop of Mercia, based in Chester around 669AD. The author Daniel Defoe described the Moss as 'too terrible to contemplate, for it will support neither man nor beast; however, reclamation work on parts of the Moss first began in 1793. Tramways were found to be the most effective means to convey reclamation material onto the unstable land.

A mix of clay and manure was left on the moss land for about a year and then dug over by hand. Much of the peat was dug out and replaced with refuse. Later the peat was transformed into a plant fertiliser known as Humogen, at Holt Town in Manchester. The reclaimed land was used for pig rearing, poultry and producing fruit and vegetables - some of which were taken by train to Covent Garden market in London. The dumping of manure was discontinued in 1923 with the increased use of the flushing toilet. Barge deliveries of waste ceased in 1939, although other tipping continued until 1966. The light railway was sold in 1940.

Cuckooland

Cuckooland is home to an amazing collection, considered to be the best of its kind in the world. Here you will find over 600 clocks gathered by brothers Roman and Max Piekarski. The cuckoo clock industry originated in the Black Forest region of Germany and here at Tabley there are many notable and fascinating examples of the craft. Farmers supplemented their income during the long snowy winter months making the clocks. Working from patterns in brochures, they carved the things they knew well - the wild animals, birds and flowers.

The museum on Chester Road was set up twenty years ago by the brothers, who also research and restore clocks. The earliest clock on display dates from about 1850. See the mysterious 'eye' clocks and the 'cameraman's assistant'. Also on display are concert organs and old vehicles.

(Cuckooland is only open as a guided tour, by arrangement.)

Above: Legh Road, right: Gaskell Memorial Tower

The buildings of Richard Harding Watt

This unusual architecture was the product of the vision and energy of Robert Harding Watt. He was a wealthy owner of a glove-importing and manufacturing business in Manchester with branches in London and Glasgow. His warehouse at seven Piccadilly, Manchester was remembered by many because of the cote which used to attract many pigeons. His buildings were a combination of styles and much influenced by architecture he had seen on his travels around the world. He particularly loved the history and the buildings of Italy but he also combined it with design from the arts and crafts movement as well as integrating segments of buildings pulled down in Manchester.

His unorthodox style was not to the liking of architectural commentator Nikolaus Pevsner who was generally dismissive of it, but it is precisely this quirkiness which has caught the attention and admiration of many.

Watt had many different interests and pursuits and from an early age he had sketched and kept journals. These journals

have been preserved and the earliest entry is a drawing of Morecambe when he was about ten. On census forms, Watts always stated that he was born in Manchester, however there is no record of his birth in the city and his parents were said to be Boers. Watt did not seem to know many details about his family background because, on his wedding certificate, he left unanswered the name and profession of his father. It is believed that Watt inherited enough from his parents' South African mining shares to travel and to set up the glove business.

Richard Harding Watt

Watt enlisted the help of four architects but invariably there was disagreement over his ideas and methods. He often changed his mind during construction to the great frustration of builders and craftsmen and one of his contractors became so upset that he threatened to shoot him after being made to rebuild a tower three times. Because he was of independent means, he was used to getting his own way and this made him unpopular in some quarters with his obsessive drive for change.

He tried to share his love of art, music and writing with those in his employment by setting up libraries and meeting-places where they could enjoy the arts. He also campaigned for better housing conditions in Knutsford. He wrote in a report in 1899 'it was the duty of

all well-to-do citizens that they interest themselves in the welfare of their poorer neighbours'. This passion for the finer things of life can be seen in the many inscriptions on his buildings which seek to uplift and remind people of our history and literary and religious heritage. He wanted to influence every part of the lives of his employees, taking an active interest in their welfare. This meant he might come to an employee's home not only to check on their health but also to see if they were keeping it well-decorated and tidy.

Inevitably his character and frenetic activity made him stand out in Knutsford and he was perhaps misunderstood by some. Britain was at war with the Boers during his life-time and that may also have influenced some people's perception of him. He once confided that he felt people treated him as a fool and yet he believed he had always tried to better their lives. He often quoted a speech from Cromwell which seemed to sum up his philosophy on life, 'Relieve the oppressed, hear the groans of the poor in England, reform the abuses. If there be any of these that make many poor to make a few rich, that suits not the commonwealth'.

Watts moved to Knutsford from Bowdon in 1895 to live at 'The Croft'. This was quite conventional in design, but his later creations along the west side of Legh Road were a spectacular combination of

Left: The Ruskin Rooms, Drury Lane, off King Street

Middle: Inscriptions on the Gaskell Memorial Tower, King Street

Above: Legh Road

architectural styles and materials. The villas were to prove popular with people with business interests in Manchester who commuted on the new train service. At the rear of the site, for the exclusive use of the house owners, is Sanctuary Moor with wetland and lake, and the Lily - England's smallest river.

'Aldwarden Hill' has in its grounds the porter's lodge from the former Old Infirmary in Manchester. 'Lakeside' is considered to be the most impressive, and includes interior features such as internal doors from Manchester Royal Infirmary and an inlaid oak floor from St Ann's Church in the city. The columns in the porch of the 'Round House' are thought to be from Walthier House in Lancashire. 'Broad Terraces' incorporates many items taken from salvaged buildings. The folly in the garden is thought to have been used as an aviary. 'The Croft' had a bell above Watt's bedroom window which rang at 7am to awaken his domestic staff and to alert the laundry employees he would soon be on his way.

His love of nature and wildlife is reflected in his work with recesses in walls for birds to perch and shelter from the rain. There was a bird sanctuary on his property along with a reptile house built into the side of the hill, and with gravestones of his favourite horses. Legh Road featured in Steven Speilberg's 'Empire of the Sun' (1987) when it became

the European quarter in 1940s Shanghai. 'High Moorland Lodge' is seen in a shot where Europeans were taken away on a truck.

The Drury Lane laundry, built by Watt on the site of the old tannery in 1899, made an astonishing sight from the Moor with its minarets, domes and a tower inspired by a similar structure he had seen in Damascus. It incorporated workers' accommodation with ironwork balconies. Watt was a great admirer of the work and philosophy of John Ruskin and named the adjoining building after him. It opened three years later with a library and meeting areas for the laundry workers.

The Gaskell Memorial Tower and King's Coffee House proved to be hisfinal project and was typical of his unique style which he thought of as 'British architecture', in spite of its Mediterranean appearance. The project faced opposition because two run-down properties had to be demolished. It incorporated a tower with a bust of Mrs Gaskell, many inscriptions and columns in the court-yard from the demolished St Peter's church in Manchester. Mrs Gaskell was born in Knutsford and immortalised the town in her novel 'Cranford'. Three bells in the tower rang on the day it officially opened in 1907, although they have since been removed. The Coffee

House was intended by Watt to be a non-profit making venture for the town where the workers could relax and eat fresh-ly- baked bread and cakes. But within a few years it became a hotel, which one guest, the author John Galsworthy in 1910, described as 'The most comfortable hotel he had ever stayed in'.

Watt waited many years to marry Mary Armitage, the daughter of a well-known Cheshire JP in 1906. It is claimed that neither his wife nor her family was impressed with Watt's distinctive buildings. Five years later he closed his glove business and trav-elled around Britain and Europe with his wife.

His sudden death in 1913 drew much public interest. He was being driven to Knutsford Station to meet a friend when he called the coach-driver to stop. By the time the coach had halted, Watt had fallen onto the road, fracturing his skull and died a few hours later at his home. At the inquest, a witness had seen Watt opening the door of the carriage before it had stopped. It also was revealed that he was being treated for a heart condition and had suffered recent bouts of dizziness. A verdict of accidental death was recorded.

The coffee house was rented to Knutsford Council in memory of Richard Harding Watt by his widow in 1914. The building is a fitting tribute to Watt, who tried hard to improve the lives of the poor and within ten years of arriving in the town his architec-tural oddities had transformed it for ever.

Left: Gaskell memorial tower
Top: Inscription on the Coffee House
Above: 'Lakeside' Legh Road

Opposite page:
Top: Legh Road
Below: The old laundry, Drury Lane

AA box, Mere Corner

The once familiar sight of the black and yellow telephone box is now a rarity. Call box 372 at Mere Corner became a listed building in 1987. It was refurbished in the 1950s style in 1995.

The present box at Mere is a replica as the original was completely destroyed in a road accident during the early hours of 21 December 1997. By the time the AA had been notified and arrived at the scene the following January, every trace of the box, including the logo sign and telephone, had disappeared. Because of its listed building status, a new fully operational box was erected on 9 April 1998 costing £6000. While some boxes have been taken over by other organizations, this is one of fifteen still owned by the AA.

The box is thought to date back to the 1930s, but the site had belonged to the AA since the early 1920s when it became one of the first petrol stations in the country. This service, along with an all-night telephone point, was exclusively for AA members. Up to this time, motorists bought their petrol in cans. Other companies soon copied the American practice of service stations.

Mere Corner had the dubious honour of being Britain's most congested point on the roads in a traffic survey conducted in August 1934 with over 113,000 vehicles in 77 hours. Before improvements were introduced, it was the scene of many serious accidents.

There were over 1000 AA boxes after they were introduced in 1911, but only about 20 remain today. Some have been relocated, including several to museums. They were originally intended as shelters and known as sentry boxes for watchmen who could provide help. Uniformed patrol men would salute motorists who displayed the AA badge, as they passed by.

Later, the boxes became places where AA members, issued with keys, could phone for help and also find emergency items such as fire extinguishers and maps. The decline in use of the 'lighthouses of the road' began in the 1960s and no further boxes were made after 1967. Improvements were made to the appearance of the boxes and then phones on posts were introduced in the 1980s before the network shut down in 2002.

CHESHIRE ARCHIVES

**Photographs
from the
Tabley Tower
visitors' book**

Tabley tower

The folly tower on an island at Tabley Mere was built around 1790, in the grounds of Tabley House. The tower features in two paintings by the great English artist JW Turner, who stayed at Tabley in 1808, entitled 'A Windy Day' and 'Tabley a Calm Morning'.

The top floor of the tower was used for duck shooting and also it was rumoured where owner Sir John Fleming Leicester kept a mistress. It was publicly acknowledged that he installed one of his women, Emily St Clare, at his London home as well as in his country residence. The Morning Post reported that Leicester had encouraged Emily, who was fifteen, to run away from her London boarding school to be with him. In the records of Tabley, there is a reference to an estimate for wall-papering 'Miss St Clare's Dressing Room'. Another document states that a room in the tower (dimensions 13ft 5ins) was to be papered.

Later, Leicester Warrens used the Mere and tower for more innocent purposes. Cuthbert Leicester Warren kept the Tabley Tower visitors' book (1917-

1921) which recorded happy family times. Some of the events are seen through the eyes of his only daughter Margaret, then in her teens, who used the tower as a playhouse and invited people over for tea and fishing in the boats Ark and Rainbow. Poems in the visitors' book refer to the tower as 'Margaret's tower' and describe her as the 'chatelaine' or hostess of the isle.

The ownership of the house and estate passed from the Leicester family to Manchester University in 1976. Today the tower, which has an impressive oak staircase, is in poor structural condition.

(The Mere and tower are closed to the public. The Tabley House collection and tea rooms have limited opening hours).

Warburton toll bridge

This is the only road and bridge in the region where you have to pay for access. Although the bridge crosses the Manchester Ship Canal, the toll is paid for using the old bridge over the dried-up bed of the river Irwell. The bridge, built in 1863, replaced an earlier bridge. Before that, people crossed by the nearby Hollins ferry. Some of the bridge iron-work over the river can be seen near to the toll house. The new bridge over the canal, built in 1894, is said to be of the same cantilever construction as Scotland's Forth Bridge. Close by where the old river branched off the canal, is the site of the landing stage where night soil from Manchester was brought to spread on Warburton's fields.

Almost home

This wayside sign on Brooklands Road reminded the wealthy Victorian banker, Samuel Brooks, as he was travelling back, that he was getting close to his home - Prospect House in Hale. Probably it was more of a reminder to the local population of who owned much of the land in the vicinity. Brooks had created a coach route - Brook's Drive and Brooklands between his 32-acre estate in Hale and the nearest station - naturally named after him. He was born in Whalley, near Clitheroe and named his new gentleman's estate, Whalley Range after it. There was a toll here - named of course Brooks' Bar. Brooks, to his credit, was forever reclaiming land for development. He was reported to have said 'Money is like muck - no use unless it is well spread!' His wealth earned him the nickname of 'Ow'd stink o'brass'.

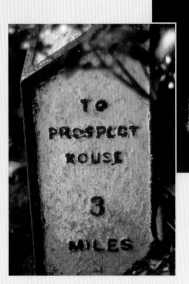

AS SAINT GEORGE IN ARMED ARRAY
DOTH THE FIERY DRAGON SLAY
SO MAYST THOU WITH MIGHT NO LES
SLAY THAT DRAGON DRUNKENNESS

Arley Rhyming Signs

Rowland Egerton-Warburton, owner of the Arley Hall estate for around 60 years up to 1891, was the writer of various signs in verse. He was a keen poet and huntsman and composed a book of hunting songs in 1834 which was so popular it ran to eight editions.

His 'Epigrams and Humorous Verses', published in 1867, was written under the name of 'Rambling Richard'. Another book of his hunting songs in 1855 had drawings by the famous illustrator 'Phiz'. Other work included 'Twenty-Two Sonnets' in 1883, and 'Arley in Idleness' - a collection of his verses which he had printed.

His work is to be seen on three sign posts around the property and over the entrance to the hall which he rebuilt. This reads 'This gate is free to all good men and true. Right welcome though if worthy to pass through'.

There is more of his work in the Tudor Barn restaurant next to two family crests with the inscription 'If proud thou be of ancestors for worth or wisdom famed. So live that they, if now alive, would not of thee be shamed'. At nearby Great Budworth, where Warburton helped to create one of Cheshire's most picturesque villages, his sign over the entrance to the George and Dragon warns of the potential evils of drink. Inside the Running Pump, at the bottom of the hill is another of his verses to remind us of the unending goodness of the Almighty.

Elephant burial

An early guide claims an elephant was buried beneath Chester Road at Stretford. No date or further details are given, but years ago there were many travelling circuses. Also there was a veterinary surgeon, JB Parkinson, nearby on Dane Road. A photograph shows elephants there during Boer War celebrations in 1902.

The Great Stone

Situated on Chester Road just outside Gorse Hill Park, it is also known as the Plague Stone. This is because the two hollowed out areas were reputedly used during the plagues between 1348 and 1665 to disinfect coins brought by incoming traders. It was previously situated in Great Stone Road until 1925. The millstone grit stone is similar to others around the region - see Robin Hood's Picking Rods for the possible origins.

Church gate

This unusual self-closing lychgate is at St Mary's Rostherne. It was built in 1640 and operates with a weight hanging from the rope. 'Lych' comes from the Saxon for corpse, because the covered gateway was used as the spot by corpse bearers to rest the coffin while the priest said prayers. From this has grown the superstition that brides should not enter through this place of death.

At the rear of the church, set into a wall, is an ancient carved head that is said to have been recovered from the Mere.

TRAFFORD LOCAL STUDIES & ARCHIVES

The bravest street in the country

The plaque, put up in 2009, reminds us of the grim toll that the Great War took on so many of the inhabitants of this street. King George famously described it as 'the bravest little street'. Many of its inhabitants were Irish immigrants, often ten sharing cramped accommodation. The street was demolished in the 1960s to make way for a car park and new housing. A roll of honour of those who gave their lives is now on a memorial at the corner of St Margarets Road and Dunham Road.

TRAFFORD COUNCIL

CHAPEL STREET ALTRINCHAM

From just 60 houses, 161 men volunteered in the Great War 1914-1918
29 were killed.

Recognised and praised by King George V

Warburton Souling play

The performance has been described as a play of death and revival and although similar to the mumming play, its origins are probably taken from 18th century pamphlets known as Chapbooks. The play, which has lots of music, action and humour is performed at several venues in early November - beginning and ending at the Saracen's Head pub, Warburton. The original plays were probably performed by the less well-off and there was a begging song at the end requesting ale and money to help the performers survive the winter.

The custom of performing this and similar traditional plays began to die out at the beginning of the 1900s and the 1938 performance of the Warburton play was to be the last for many years. The Bollin Morris revived the play in 1978 at the Saracen's Head and the tradition has been continued by a group with morris connections and others.

The play includes a horse character and the head was traditionally buried in the grounds in the Saracen's Head until it was required the following year.

Barton Swing Aqueduct

The moveable aqueduct carries the Bridgewater Canal over the Manchester Ship Canal. It opened in 1894 and replaced the Barton aqueduct designed by James Brindley. The swing aqueduct is the only one ever built and is still in use. It is regarded as an engineering masterpiece and distinguished visitors to the area were often brought to see it in action.

Above: A walk-way on the western side of the aqueduct is seen in earlier photographs.

Below: The two bridges in open postion to allow ships through.

The waterway within the structure incorporates an iron trough weighing 1,400 tons when full, 19ft wide and 6ft deep. Gates at either end control the flow of water to the Bridgewater Canal. It is supported by 64 rollers on a circular platform. Below there are two openings of 90ft and 60 ft for vessels on the Ship Canal to pass either side of the island containing the brick control tower.

Early leakage problems on the aqueduct were found by divers to be caused by a pick with a wooden shaft and other items floating in the water preventing the water-tight gates from closing properly.

The aqueduct is next to the Barton Road swing bridge on Redclyffe Road, which is also controlled from the control tower. When ships approach, the two bridges rotate to line up on the island.

Knutsford
Post Office

The old grocer's and post office on Mobberley Road with a date mark of 1881 was a daily reminder to local inhabitants of the rewards of hard work and sacrifice. Richard Harding Watt, who lived in Legh Road opposite, will have noted these sayings and he also incorporated writings and texts on his buildings.

THINK OF EASE BUT WORKON

NO GAINS WITHOUT PAINS

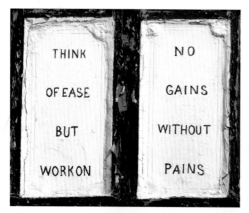

THINK
OF EASE
BUT
WORKON

NO
GAINS
WITHOUT
PAINS

GREAT BUSINESS MUST
OUR MISSION IS TO SELL
YOURS TO QUICKLY BUY

BE WROUGHT TO DAY
WE'LL DO OUR PART FULL WELL
IF YOU'L ONLY LET US TRY

WARRINGTON & WIGAN

Lymm Tower House

The water tower, off Higher Lane, was built over 130 years ago and in 1997 it was bought to be adapted into a home. The owner, a TV production company director, decided on a wrap-around glass and steel extension at the base of tower. It was designed by architects Ellis Williams who were responsible for the Baltic Centre at Gateshead. The new home, took eight years to build, and has won many awards and featured in advertisements and a TV series. The owner said that he loved having a gin and tonic on the roof garden on an early summer's evening and watching the traffic struggling along the M60.

Unusual rocks by Lymm Dam

Just below St Mary's Church are the curious rocks which are only found here and at Thurston Hill on the Wirral. The rounded steps were formed 10,000 years ago when Cheshire was covered by ice and then eroded as fast-flowing water melted beneath. The deep cuts in the rocks are known as Nye Channels.

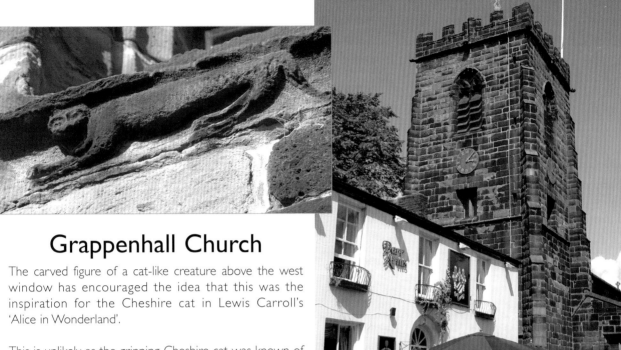

Grappenhall Church

The carved figure of a cat-like creature above the west window has encouraged the idea that this was the inspiration for the Cheshire cat in Lewis Carroll's 'Alice in Wonderland'.

This is unlikely, as the grinning Cheshire cat was known of by 1792 - many years before Carroll's book (1865). It has also been suggested that the Grappenhall cat is part of a coat of arms, and possibly a pun on the name or logo of local family Robert De Boydell of Caterich who built the church and owned other property in the parish and placed the cat carving on the church tower between 1529 and 1539.

Carroll no doubt visited the church because he grew up in nearby Daresbury and would have seen cheese being made into animal shapes, including cats. However, at the age of eleven he went to live at Croft on Tees, where his father, the Rector, would sit on a stone seat built into the wall, which also had a carved face of a cat or lion. There are cat-like carvings in other churches around the country including St Christopher's Church, Pott Shrigley. It is possible that the carvings have pagan associations.

Yet another theory for the origins of the Cheshire cat, is that the wolf's head on the Earls of Chester's coat of arms had been mistaken for a cat. At Ringway, the inn was originally known as 'The Red Lion', but because of the painting on the sign it became known as 'The romping kitlin (kitten)'. This has since evolved to its present name of 'The Romper'. Through misunderstanding of images, names can change and the origins of the grinning Cheshire cat remain uncertain.

Scratch dial on the church

Grappenhall church also has the remains of several scratch dials. These are a form of sun dial which indicated when the bell-ringer should ring the church bell. The presence of more than one suggests that the maker was trying to find the best place. The practice started in Norman times and they were in use until the sixteenth century.

The 'Golden Gates'

The gates on Sankey Street were originally offered to Sandringham Palace, but when Queen Victoria inspected them at Rotten Row in Hyde Park, London, she rejected them because of a statue of Oliver Cromwell immediately behind them. As Cromwell had signed the death warrant of her ancestor King Charles the First, she wanted nothing to do with the gates and they were returned to Ironbridge. The cast-iron gates had been made at Coalbrookdale for the 1862 International Exhibition and were regarded as the finest of their type in the country.

Frederick Monks, a local foundry owner and member of Warrington council, saw the gates on frequent visits to Ironbridge. He offered them as a gift to Warrington and they were officially presented to the town in 1895, replacing a high brick wall which had previously surrounded the town hall. The statue of Cromwell which had so deeply offended Queen Victoria was erected at Bridge Foot in the town. Four years later, an impressive ornamental fountain was built behind the gates, but this was taken down during the last War. The gates only became 'golden' in 1997 when the black gates were repainted in the royal colours for the Queen's Silver Jubilee.

Cromwell statue

Warrington Transporter Bridge

Spanning 187 ft over the River Mersey, it was built to take rail vehicles between the sites owned by Crossfield and Sons chemical and soap works. It is one of only four transporter bridges built in this country. The transporter began operating in 1916 and could take loads up to 18 tons. In 1940 it was modified to take road vehicles and the tonnage limit later increased to 30 tons.

The first transporter on the site was built around 1905 in connection with the new cement works. The present bridge was taken out of service around 1964 and is now owned by the local council. The structure, sometimes known as the Bank Quay Transporter, is a scheduled ancient monument but is in urgent need of restoration.

The transporter is on the private site of the PQ Corporation but it can be viewed from the eastern side of the River Mersey, via a road which goes past the karting centre off Slutchers Lane.

Haigh Windmill

The windmill was built to pump water from two ponds in an adjoining field to Haigh Brewery reservoir in 1845. A windmill, rather than a steam engine was chosen in order to avoid any further undesirable black smoke blowing across Lord Crawford's Haigh Hall. Also it made a picturesque addition to the landscape. Surplus water from the working was piped to the hall and some of the homes on the estate.

In 1872 the local authority took over the responsibility of providing the water supply to the area and by 1895 the windmill was not used. It fell into disrepair over the years but some restoration took place in the 1970s and 1990s. A £50,000 grant from the Lottery Heritage fund in 2011 enabled brickwork and a sail to be repaired on Greater Manchester's last surviving windmill which is within the Haigh Hall estate.

Rectory Garden Centre

This is a garden centre like no other, in the Greater Manchester area, and probably throughout the country. It is the ongoing creation of owner Kevin Duffy, who has been working on it for over thirty years. It began as a neglected allotment which he took over, and through the years it grew from a place where Kevin sold a few plants and cuttings into a commercial garden centre. He now lives on the site in a bungalow.

With the help of his son he has transformed the site into this unusual slightly fairy tale world with a surreal twist. At every turn there is a surprise for the visitor. It is an ever-changing scene with a mixture of man-made and natural features. There are curious buildings, lots of figures and heads but also ducks and of course plants.

The place is a folly-seeker's paradise with towers, monuments and quirky buildings. They are all constructed using reclaimed materials which Kevin either finds or is given. Items have come from Liverpool docks, a nearby hospital and even Bob the donkey's grave stone. There are also several interiors to explore - a convincing chapel, and another room with a strange assortment of mannequins. One of Kevin's distinctive themes is the mysterious head or figure peering through windows and gaps. It is important to look around carefully, because there are many little witty items that you may otherwise miss.

Kevin is self-taught; he started his working life in the mills and then later performed his music with his wife Pat in pubs and clubs. But his passion for building and creating knows no limits and he visits stately homes around the north of England for inspiration. Some of his influences come from much further afield using pattern and design from South America and the Arab world. His wife died some years ago, and she is fondly remembered in a specially created monument, complete with angel.

His technique for the building facades is to use reclaimed interior doors which he covers in mesh and then renders in sand and cement. To keep the plants on the site well watered, Kevin has dug a number of wells which are made into features.

Kevin's creation has featured on regional TV and although some have likened it to Portmeirion, I think it has a unique character which will delight and fascinate visitors. Income from the centre goes towards further developing this curious 'other world' in Recory Road, North Ashton near Wigan.

Rectory Garden Centre

SALFORD

Phil's folly

The 40ft-tall lighthouse is at Monton on the banks of the Bridgewater Canal at Eccles. Completed in 2004, it cost £20,000 and took four years to build. The biggest expense was for the 10ft deep foundation of concrete. Its creator, Phil Austin, lived in a boat by the surgery and was thinking of settling in Wales when he was offered the land which is part of a conservation area and had the idea of building a lighthouse.

The interior is not fully completed, but it includes the couch and carpet from the BBCs 'Northwest Tonight' programme and a wooden staircase from a disused Birmingham church. Phil plans to have murals depicting the themes of underwater, through to space on the walls. The light came from a lightship.

Phil is a member of the British Lighthouse Keepers Association. He has noticed that the usual reaction when boaters see it for the first time is to grab a camera. He even overheard one local claim it was there when he was younger. There is thought to be one other inland lighthouse in Leicestershire.

Phil has won awards from Tango and Bric Vic for the unusual building. He is currently restoring 'Victoria R', a replica of the boat which was used for Queen Victoria's visit to Worsley in 1851.

Top: The Eccles coat of arms curiously features a lighthouse

Above: Phil and the old BBC sofa

The clock struck thirteen

The clock at St Mark's, Worsley strikes thirteen times at one o'clock. It used to be at the Duke of Bridgewater's workyard at Worsley, where it was the signal for his workforce to return to work after lunch. The Duke had noticed that, although the workers stopped promptly at noon, they were not so quick to return at the one o'clock bell. Excuses were made that they had not heard the single bell because of the general noise in the yard and so the thirteen bells were introduced. The clock, with its unique chiming mechanism was removed to the church in 1946.

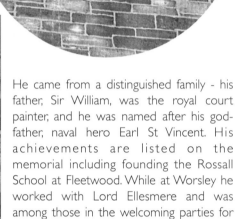

At the side of the church is the so-called 'unfinished grave'. The unusual monument with fragments of stone is a memorial to St Vincent Beechey 1806-1899 who was vicar of Worsley for twenty-two years.

He came from a distinguished family - his father, Sir William, was the royal court painter, and he was named after his godfather, naval hero Earl St Vincent. His achievements are listed on the memorial including founding the Rossall School at Fleetwood. While at Worsley he worked with Lord Ellesmere and was among those in the welcoming parties for royal visits in 1851 and 1857. He was also President of the Manchester Photographic Society. Even at the age of ninety he was taking two or three Sunday services. When he died three years later, he was thought to be oldest clergyman in the Church of England.

Polly's grave

The memorial is in the grounds of the Cock Hotel, Worsley. Polly the pig was kept by the publican Mrs Alice Taylor in 1902 when there was a farm attached to the premises. The Taylor family managed the pub from around 1890 to 1908. Polly was something of a visitor attraction and enjoyed a jug of beer - possibly fortifying her to produce so many piglets. She is said to have died of cirrhosis and had to be shot. The headstone is said not to be the actual resting place of Polly.

Mark Addy

His rescue exploits began at the age of fourteen - even before he could swim. He saved one person by wading into the water and another by sitting on a floating plank. Later he was the landlord of the Boathouse inn on the Salford side of the river Irwell and

established a reputation for saving people from the murky waters. If anyone called out out for help he would immediately leave his customers, a family gathering, or his bed to dive into the river. Once he was returning from a funeral when he was told there was a child in the river. He immediately dived in and rescued the little boy,. His suit was ruined and his watch irrepairable but a life saved was more important.

The people he rescued often strongly resisted his efforts. They were half-drunk or suicidal and tried to drag Addy down with themselves. Spectators on the river bank would urge him to save himself, but he always thought it was his duty, day or night, to bring them to safety.

Top: One of the cups awarded to Mark Addy

Below: the Mark Addy Bridge, off Woden Street

His bravery was rewarded with a number of honours, including the Albert Medal - later renamed The Victoria Cross and silver and gold medals from the Salford Hundred Humane Society. In 1878 he was awarded 200 guineas for his brave deeds at a banquet given in his honour at Salford Town Hall. In the tribute speech it was said 'To plunge into ordinary water requires pluck, but to plunge into that miserable sink, the Irwell requires heroicqualities, such as we cannot value too highly'.

His life-saving feats continued up to Whit Monday 1889 when he fell ill after a rescuing a young lad. The years of going into the heavily polluted water finally took its toll and he died of TB the following year aged fifty two. Just before he died he said he valued the joy and the gratitude of the brothers and sisters of the boy from his last rescue more than all the medals he had received.

The pole at its previous site

Totem pole

It was given as a gift to Manchester Liners in 1969 as a symbol of the good trading partnership between Canada and the City. Carved out of Columbian pine, it stood outside Furness House where very few people would see it. The pole is carved with animals and figures who have significance to the Kwakiutl Indians of Vancouver Island. The eagle represents the ruler of the skies, the killer whale is the master of the seas and the raven is a messenger. At the foot of the pole the chief is holding symbols of power and wealth.

The pole was taken down in 2006 for health and safety reasons, and stored in a depot at Felixstowe. It has now been refurbished by a Salford company and discussions are taking place where to re-erect it.

Irwell floods

Flooding from the River Irwell on Friday 16th November 1866 was described as the worst on record. The obelisk in Peel Park, erected in 1867, indicates that the waters reached a height of 8ft 6ins at this point. Three days of rain had caused the river to rise 14ft above its normal height. The head gardener at Peel Park had to be rescued from the top floor of his home, along with his family, by means of a ladder into a boat. At seven in the morning, the park paths were usable but within an hour they were three feet under water.

Riverside factories and mills were overwhelmed and around seven hundred people were rescued by boat from roofs and upper storeys in Salford and Manchester. Some of the boats had been borrowed from the Belle Vue lake. 3500 homes and 40 factories were flooded, and three people lost their lives.

Within four days of the disaster, Salford Council were instructing the public to hand in anything found on the river bank to the Police Office at the Town Hall and had opened a fund in aid of the victims. Local companies were advertising their furniture and upholstery repair services for flood-damaged items.

A flood in October 1870 reached 4ft 3ins, which is also marked.

Worsley mines

This is the entrance to an extensive network of underground canals known as the 'Navigable Level' stretching nearly 52 miles. They were built for Francis Egerton, the third Duke of Bridgewater to bring out coal from his mines for transportation along his canal to Manchester.

The Act of Parliament for the canal stipulated that the coal was to be sold at a maximum of two and a half pence per hundredweight for a period of forty years. Work started in 1759 on the route which starts at Delph in Worsley and runs in a northwesterly direction to Farnworth.

Apart from the main 41,980yd long tunnel there was also a higher level canal, thirty-five yards above, to work other seams between Walkden and Farnworth. Coal-laden boats were taken from the upper level to the main navigation level by means of a lock. Boats were then lowered onto a trolley which took them down a hundred and fifty-yard incline.

By 1820 the upper level and the inclined plane ceased to be used but were still maintained. The water, when it flows out of the tunnels, is a distinctive orange colour, originating from the iron in the rocks.

The volume of canal traffic caused jams at the tunnel entrance and so in 1771 work started on a second entrance thirty yards to the west. As there was no space to turn around, boats were purpose-built with both ends shaped as bows so as to be able to travel in either direction.

The old mine entrance
as seen from Worsley Road.

This great feat of engineering was viewed with enormous curiosity and many people journeyed to Worsley to visit the Duke of Bridgewater's 'sough'. King Christian of Denmark visited in 1768, when he and his fifty courtiers were taken through in nine boats.

In 1910 there were eight collieries and there was optimism about the future. They had invested in new equipment and processes and there were large reserves of coal. However, changes in ownership and the coming Depression brought the closure of many pits. By the time of coal nationalisation in 1947, only two 'Bridgewater Pits' remained. Mosley became the last pit linked to the system which was filled in and closed in 1968 and and the Navigable Level abandoned. The last official sailing along the canal was an inspection in 1999 which reported that the tunnels were still in good condition. Over forty miles of canal still remain.

The mines are closed to the public.

BOLTON

Pigeon tower

It was a lookout tower, built around 1910, with three levels. The first two floors were bird houses, while on the third is a sitting room where Lady Leverhulme is said to have spent many hours indulging in her interests of embroidery and music and enjoying the panoramic views. Her husband's passion for continual building and development meant she found it difficult to call anywhere 'home' and it was possibly here that she found peace and refuge. She once commented that they were rarely free from the presence of workmen.

But even here we have an indication of Lord Leverhulme's restless pursuit of improvement. Over the fireplace there are the initials of William Hesketh and Elizabeth Ellen Lever along with the motto 'To change or to fear I spurn'. Access to the floors was via a winding stone staircase, which can be seen by the semi-circular tower on the building.

A 250ft-long screen with pigeon holes and nesting boxes running below the tower, along with bird houses situated throughout the estate, helped to introduce sound and life to this sometimes rather bleak place. By 1974 the Rivington estate was managed by the North West Water Authority and the following year it cost £5000 to restore the Pigeon Tower, which was then in poor condition.

Above top: The Bolton 'Lake District' from the tower site
Above: Pigeon holes
Right: Pigeon tower

Lever's Bridge

Lord Leverhulme made his fortune through the production of Sunlight soap. He owned the estate at Rivington and had wanted a seven-arched bridge over the Horwich-Chorley road for some time. His chief stone mason was unable to understand how it could be done as the road was only wide enough for one arch. However, Leverhulme had already seen a bridge like this on his travels and the mason soon found himself on a plane with his lordship to Nigeria to see for himself. The replica design for the unusual bridge over the gorge at Rivington was completed around 1910.

Lord Leverhulme

Rivington Pike

The square tower on the Pike was built in 1733 at a cost of £85 for John Andrews, the owner of the Rivington Manor Estate. It was thought to represent a mark of ownership following earlier disputes and was built on the site of a beacon. Stone from the old beacon, once part of a chain stretching across the country in the 12th century, was used in the building of the tower. Rock from the nearby River Douglas was also built into the base of the tower.

At the time of Henry VII the site was known locally as 'Riven Pike'. The beacon had been made ready in 1588 to warn that the Spanish Armada were in the English Channel. Again in 1804 the beacon was prepared when it was feared that Napoleon's army would invade England. The beacons were made up of huge pieces of timber, barrels of tar, pitch and resin and wood chips and shavings. Watchmen were employed at the site to make sure the huge pile of inflammable material was not set off prematurely causing unnecessary alarm and panic. After the emergencies had passed, much of the timber was taken away by locals and weathering gradually cleared the rest.

Above: The Pike.

Inside the tower, the floor is flagged, there is a fireplace and a cellar. It was rarely used except for grouse-shooting parties from Rivington Hall as a hunting lodge, when it became a 'dining-hall for the sportsman of the moors, its grey walls echoing to the drawing of corks and the jovial laugh of those assembled for refreshment of the inner man beneath its roof'.

A later owner, WH Lever, gave it to Bolton Corporation in 1900 for public use. By 1967 the land and the nearby reservoirs were owned by Liverpool Corporation. Because of the tower's poor condition, due to vandalism, they proposed to demolish it and have an inscribed stone at the spot. Following protests, the tower was gifted to Chorley Rural District Council who agreed to fund the £1000 restoration costs and have continued to maintain it.

Beyond is Winter Hill where there is a memorial known as Scotsman's Stump, by the transmitters. It is an iron post with a plaque to George Henderson, a Scottish merchant who was shot dead here in 1838. A local man stood trial but was later acquitted. The post was erected in 1912.

Bonfires next to the Pike have been lit on Royal occasions and to celebrate the end of the First World War. The annual Pike Fair on Good Friday and Pike Race on Easter Saturday remain popular events. Also, the Christian tradition to visit the site on Good Friday continues to be observed. From the Pyke, in good weather conditions, the Isle of Man, Blackpool Tower and the Welsh mountains are to be seen.

Liverpool Castle

It stands on the eastern shore of Lower Rivington Reservoir, which was owned by Liverpool Corporation and built to resemble the ruins of Liverpool Castle. Lord Leverhulme thought that the Coblowe site at Rivington closely resembled that at Liverpool and would be an appropriate link between the two areas. The castle at Rivington was to be a replica of Liverpool's fortifications in the period after the Civil War. The old ruins had been used as a shelter for the homeless before it was demolished in 1725.

Using local stone, work began at Rivington in 1912 to plans drawn up by a local historian. Only a few people worked there and it was still unfinished at the time of Leverhulme's death in 1925. Work continued for a further five years to complete the scaled-down version of the fortress. After weathering over the years, the site now has the look of an authentic ruin. However, the public are warned about climbing its walls which are unstable.

Blackrod folly

The tower is built into the walls of Arley Hall kitchen garden and grounds, which belong to Wigan Golf Club. There used to be fruit trees and vegetables here and it is thought to be a ventilation shaft for an underground heating system to encourage extra growth of the produce (See Abney Hall, Cheadle for a similar system). It is known as the watch tower and may also have been used as a bell tower.

The folly is in private grounds and can be viewed by prior arrangement with Wigan Golf Club.

Firewatchers' post

This must have been a particularly hazardous spot on top of the old gas works at New Holder Street, Bolton. The Fire Watcher Service began in 1940, but within a year it had been reorganised into the Fire Guard. As well as looking out for fires, their role was to put out fires and incendiary bombs with stirrup pumps where possible. They could also report enemy aircraft activity. Men between the ages of 18 and 60, unless exempted had to register for service. They then underwent training including how to walk on roofs. Later, women were also encouraged to register. By November 1943, as the enemy's threat receded, firewatching was reduced in numbers of personnel and hours - mainly restricted to watching during the hours of darkness.

Bradshaw chapel tower

The tower is the survivng part of the former 16th century Chapel of ease church of St Maxentius. Restoration was completed in 1986 along with its rededication. It still retains its bell.

BURY

Nabbs House 'images'

The spectacular garden summer-house folly known as 'The Images' was built around 1835 by the owner John Turner. It is within the grounds of a house on Brandlesholme Road, Greenmount. Turner was a wealthy eccentric industrialist and spent most of his time on the moors either shooting game or excavating coal with the help of his gamekeeper. Inside, the summer-house was panelled in oak and occasionally Turner and his employee had binges here that went on for several days, or they used it as a retiring room for smoking and port.

'The Images' probably referred to the many gargoyles on the building and around the garden which were said to be the unflattering carvings of Greenmount people Turner did not like. They are not dissimilar to the carvings on the nearby Tottington Dungeon. One of the most impressive carvings depicts a man with a gun and a dog by his feet - presumably either Turner or his gamekeeper. Just to be totally unsociable Turner arranged various water spouts around the property to give a soaking to uninvited callers. There is also a passage, once lined with coloured glass, connecting the summer-house to the house. The summer-house is currently being restored.

The summer-house is within private grounds and not open to the public.

Above: The passage way from the summer-house to the main house.

Left: Fireplace in the summer-house

Grant's Tower

The tower was built around 1829 in memory of the Grant family's long journey from Morayshire, Scotland to Lancashire in 1783. They came with hope of work with Richard Arkwright, the pioneer cotton spinner but that was not to happen. The family settled in Bury, eventually forming a successful calico printing and dyeing company in Ramsbottom. The Grants were responsible for several notable buildings in Ramsbottom, and also had business premises on Cannon Street, Manchester.

Two of William Grant's sons continued the business and William built the tower at 'Top of the Hoof', the site where the exhausted family shared their remaining food before going down into the Irwell valley. Brothers Daniel and William have been described as the inspiration behind Charles Dickens' characters of the Cheeryble brothers in 'Nicholas Nickleby'. There has been much discussion about whether the famous author ever met them, or if he had heard of their benevolence through friends when he visited Manchester.

Above: The present day ruins accessed from Manchester Road.
Right: Grant's tower c1900

The opening of the tower was accompanied by the Grants' usual generosity, with all the employees given the day off to celebrate. Barrels of beer and large quantities of food were taken up to the site, where there were races, games and a sing-song. The three surviving Grant brothers - William, John and Daniel, joined the fun, and two cannons were fired.

The fifty-foot-high tower commanded magnificent views across the surrounding countryside and was a popular destination for visitors and picnickers. It was open at weekends for a small admission charge to go up the four flights of 84 steps to the battlements where there was room for fifty people. Two of the turrets in the battlements were really chimneys from the rooms below. The key for the tower was kept at Top of the Hoof Farm. The tower also opened on Good Fridays and other special holidays with refreshments and swings and see-saws for the children at the nearby farm.

The job-description of a steeplejack comes from the nick-name given to James Wright who lived at the tower with his family in the 1850s. Born near Dundee in 1829 and after serving in the navy, he began repairing chimneys, steeples and monuments. But instead of scaffolding, he used a kite to fix ropes to the top of structures. It is thought he had learned the technique in his early years in Egypt where a 100ft-tall granite column known as Pompey's Pillar had been repaired in this way.

After the work was completed Wright would amaze spectators by the terrifying speed at which he would descend - at an estimated 100 miles an hour. Through this he became known as the fastest man in the world. His work was often combined with other feats and attracted vast crowds. His stunts would spectacularly end to the accompaniment of fire-works, fire balloons and fanfares. He became so famous that a letter from Edinburgh requesting his services, addressed to him as 'somewhere in England', reached Grant's Tower.

He first came to Ramsbottom to repair a factory chimney belonging to Richard Ashton and got to know the Grant brothers. When he enquired about living at the tower, he was told it was not in a fit state and had never been inhabited. However, the Grants accepted

his request and Wright wrote 'After being repaired to my satis-faction, I got it comfortably furnished and took possession along with my family, under the title of Steeple Jack of the Tower of Ramsbottom.' By 1858 he had moved to Bury.

His reputation brought him work in Belgium and New Jersey and newspapers referred to him as the 'Flying man'. But after a life-time of climbing the world's highest chimneys he died in 1902 at Dundee hospital without mention in the local newspaper .

A forester in the employ of the Grants later lived at Grants Tower with his family. Even then, there were fears for the stability of the building on this exposed site at 800 ft above sea level. During a severe storm one night the family, fearing the tower was going to collapse, vacated to nearby Nuttall further downhill. No-one ever lived at the tower after that, although Edwin Waugh, the Lancashire dialect poet, spent time at the tower while recovering from illness and wrote 'Lie thi' down laddie' after being inspired by the view from his window.

Above: The present day ruins of Grants Tower. Pieces of the battlements can be seen.

By 1914 a restoration fund was set up to meet the tower's deterio-rating condition. Ramsbottom Council finally closed the tower in 1942 because of much-needed repairs and were in negotiation with the owner, Sir Peter Grant Lawson Bart to take over its mainte-nance. Sadly before the arrangements were completed, the tower toppled and collapsed at noon on 21September 1944 with huge clouds of dust enveloping the valley. Prior to the collapse, the Home Guard were stationed here at night in case of enemy parachutists. The once-private beautiful woods on top of the hill were thought to have been decimated by fumes from the nearby chemical works.

Tottington Dungeon

It was built on to the rear of the Dungeon Pub and was used as an overnight 'cooler' for drunks. Built around 1835, it may also have been used to hold offenders temporarily before being taken into police custody. It was reputed to have replaced an earlier building where highway men were detained. The local police later took over the running of the dungeon, and the keys and handcuffs are now kept at the pub which was later rebuilt further along the road.

The Dungeon was last used around 1884. The pub has a mural featuring the dungeon, painted by a local woman who has since emigrated to Australia. During the last World War, the windows of the pub were blown out by a stray bomb, but this did not deter one of its regulars, who came in for his usual 'draught'. This rare example of a village lock-up attracted the attention of Salford Museum who wanted to relocate the Dungeon within the Lark Hill Museum street but, following local opposition, the idea was dropped.

Key and handcuffs used at the 'Dungeon'

Peel Tower

Erected in memory of Bury born Sir Robert Peel - famous as Prime Minister, founder of the modern police force and for his work in repealing the Corn Laws. It stands on Holcombe Hill and cost up to £1000 to build, through money raised by the public. The 128ft high tower, built with stone quarried from the hill and with originally 148 steps, commands impressive views over the Isle of Man, Mow Cop in Staffordshire, and Snowdonia. It officially opened in September 1852 and was managed by trustees after the hill and tower were granted a lease in perpetuity for seven shillings and sixpence a year by the owner, the Lord of the Manor - Duke of Buccleuch.

By 1929 improvements had been carried out, after another public appeal, including a new iron staircase to replace the original wooden steps and the installation of Peel's 1846 resignation speech on marble stone. The following year, a fire probably started by a visitor's lighted match or cigarette, completely destroyed the five wooden balconies within the tower. With smoke pouring out of the top, the tower resembled a mill chimney. With the nearest water supply two miles away, the fire services had to allow the fire to burn itself out. In 1935, the trustees were appealing for finances to paint the staircase and point the stonework.

The sale of light refreshments was permitted in the original agreement and the Vickers family at Holcombe Hill Farm held the concession to provide refreshments and issue admission tickets to the tower before it closed in the 1940s. Margaret Vickers recalled having to sandpaper the rusting staircases each year and whitewash the basement walls. Good Friday was an important day with many coming on an annual pilgrimage. Stalls selling pies, crisps, muffins, minerals and cigarette dispensers were set up, with help from the village, not only outside the farm but also behind the tower.

Parts of the area continue to be used as a firing range.

The hill was also the venue for the annual motorbike 'Grand National' attracting big crowds to the scramble and the tower. The old tradition of egg-rolling continues today, each Good Friday. After a service at the bottom of the hill, the egg-rolling begins mid-morning.

During the last World War, the tower and hill were guarded in case of enemy parachutists. Seven-foot high stakes were driven onto the moor to deter plane landings.

By 1947 the tower's stairs were again in poor condition and the building was closed to the public and visitor numbers to the site drastically decreased. Ownership was handed to the local district council in 1949 and the tower finally re-opened in 1985 after it had been restored and a mainly new staircase installed by Bury Council at a cost of around £40,000.

Fitzpatricks owner, Chris Law

Britain's last temperence bar

Fitzpatricks, on Bank Street, Rawtenstall, established in 1890, has always sold non-alcoholic drinks. Many temperance bars opened in the 19th century to combat the temptations of excessive drinking. It began with a Methodist cheesemaker in Preston who started the movement of signing a pledge never again to drink alcohol. Temperance bars like Fitzpatrick's sprung up all over Lancashire and Yorkshire.

People would gather for sing-songs while drinking sarsaparilla and ginger beer. Fitzpatrick's had a chain of shops and the last in the family to run the shop was Malachi. He reached the age of ninety and naturally credited his longevity to the products in his shop. He claimed he had never been ill in the last fity years of his life. The cordials are served from barrels at the old bar, with little changed from the original recipes. Also on sale are many vareties of herbs and sweets, in this step back in time.

Greenmount tower

The buildings were previously known as 'Tower Farm' and were partly used as stables for the nearby Tottington Mill Printworks. The tower originally held water in case of fire at the farm. Around sixteen carthorses were kept here to transport goods from the mill. The castellated tower and walls were built in the 1840s by the owner, Joshua Knowles, who reputedly needed to disprove local rumours that he was in financial difficulty. He also wanted it to rival the design of the gatehouse tower at Nuttall Hall farm where he had once been apprenticed to the Grant brothers of Ramsbottom.

The innovative calico print mill was the first to use an eight-colour printing machine and exhibited at the Great Exhibition in 1851. The main mill closed in 1928 and the Home Guard used the ruins as a shooting range during the last World War. The property, off Brandlesholme Road and now known as 'Tower Court', has been converted into apartments and the surrounding site landscaped.

Above: The gatehouse at Nuttall Hall

Black pudding throwing championships

The annual contest takes place on the second Sunday in September, close to the Royal Oak pub, on Bridge Street, Ramsbottom. Competitors have to dislodge, with the aid of Bury Black Puddings, as many Yorkshire puddings as they can, which are stacked on a twenty-foot high ledge. With one foot on the 'golden grid', they are allowed three attempts, throwing underarm. The black puddings, weighing 6oz, are 'swaddled' or wrapped in ladies' tights. There is a lower level of puddings for children to aim at.

The contest is said to have its origins in the Wars of the Roses era, when the two sides resorted to throwing food at each other. It is especially difficult if the day is rainy because the soaked puddings become much harder to remove. The contest draws competitors, sightseers and media crews from all round the world. The 'golden grid' is kept in a secret location for the rest of the year but on contest day it arrives via the East Lancashire Railway and is 'piped' to the Royal Oak. Winners receive a medal, a trophy and a money prize, and the proceeds from the event go a local charity.

Turton railway bridges

James Kay, the owner of Turton Tower and also director of the railway company, commissioned two footbridges over the railway line. They had to be in keeping with the rest of the estate, following the building of the Bolton to Blackburn Railway in 1847, through the grounds. They were designed by the railway company's resident engineer Terrence Wolfe Flanagan. One of them incorporates a viewing tower that would have ensured a maximum of engine smoke and steam in the face.

Walter Whitehead

Whitehead Clock Tower

The tower and gardens, opened in 1914, were built in memory of Walter Whitehead (1840-1913), an eminent Manchester surgeon. It had been arranged by his brother Henry, who was also responsible for the John Kay Memorial in Bury. Maxwell and Tuke, architects of Blackpool Tower, designed the tower in what was to be their last commission. The ornate tower, built in Portland stone, has an internal staircase to the clock and bell tower, although there is no bell. At the opening ceremony, the clock was set in motion by John, the nephew of Walter.

Walter Whitehead was born in Bury, and came from an innovative family. He was a descendant of John Kay, inventor of the flying shuttle and related to Peter Whitehead, who developed the first torpedo. From school, Walter joined his father's bleaching business but while attending chemistry lectures as part of his training he met with medical students who invited him to watch operations taking place at Manchester Infirmary.

He became so interested that, without telling his parents, he became a student at the Chatham School of Medicine and went on to become a surgeon of international renown and among his many titles he was 'President of the British Medical Association' in 1902. He was responsible for the establishment of the Manchester and Salford Hospital for Diseases of the Skin and also the first day nursery.

At the time he entered the profession in 1864, anaesthetics were a new thing and antiseptics in surgery were not known about. His success was founded on his speed and skill and his willingness to tackle risky operations. He was in great demand and his work made him wealthy. Two of his text books describing his operations made him well-known within the profession.

He was a heavy smoker and even puffed at his cigar during consultations with male patients. His hobby was yachting and he spent his weekends at Windermere. When his health deteriorated he went to live at Colwyn Bay, where he bought Flagstaff Hill and had impressive gardens designed by Thomas Mawson. It included a 'lookout' which was fitted to look like the interior of a yacht. The site is now the location of the Welsh Mountain Zoo.

The memorial and stones on Holcombe Moor.

The 'Strange' memorial

Several versions of how Ellen Strange met her death have been given over the years, but the mystery seems to have been solved by John Simpson in his book published by Helmshore Local History Society. Ellen, real name Ellen Broadley, was murdered on Holcombe Moor in 1761. An inquest at nearby Stake Farm concluded that her husband John was the perpetrator and he was sent for trial at Lancaster where he was acquitted due to lack of evidence. It was believed the couple had quarrelled earlier and that Ellen had been killed by her drunken husband as she made her way home.

After her tragic death, people began to place stones at the spot where her body had been found and this custom continues to the present day. The memorial was added close to the stones in 1978 by the local Horse and Bamboo Theatre Company for one of their performances.

Right: A Jacobean-style garden folly built in 1840 next to the grounds of Turton Tower.

Acknowledgments

MANCHESTER EVENING NEWS

Alex Britton, present owner
of the Gaddum observatory
in its previous location.
See page 16

Bibliography
2ZY to NBH by Ian Hartley
A History of Ashton-Under-Lyne and District by W Glover
Bygone Stalybridge by Samuel Hill
Curiosities of Greater Manchester by Robert Nicholls
Disley Ancient and Modern by Susan Marshall
Ellen Strange - A Moorland Mystery Explained, by John Simpson
Enterprise in Soap and Chemicals by AE Musson
History of Hyde by Thomas Middleton
Leverhulme's Rivington by MD Smith
Manchester's Narrow Gauge Railways: Chat Moss & Carrington Estates
by Robert Nicholls
Mellor's Gardens by RC Turner
Mystical Oldham by Janette Quinlan
Sam Hurst 'The Stalybridge Infant' by Mark Sheppard
Sanding: a Knutsford Custom by Joan Leach
Stalybridge Pubs 1750-1990 by Rob Magee
Tameside by C Wilkins Jones
The Black Night Rides Out by Phillip Martin Williams and David L Williams
The Fastest Man - Steeple Jack's Adventures in Lancashire by Chris Aspen
The Historic Gardens of England - Cheshire by Timothy Mowl
and Marion Mako
The Land of the Etherow by Neville T Sharpe
The Wigan Century - a History of Wigan Golf Club by Jack Winstanley

With thanks for the assistance given by the Local studies libraries and
archives at: Bolton, Bury, Cheshire, Knutsford, Macclesfield, Manchester,
Oldham, Salford, Rochdale, Stockport, Tameside, Trafford and Wigan
and the Greater Manchester Record Office

I am also grateful for the kind help, advice and information and permission
to take photographs from:

Phil Austin
Ken Bowden
Paula Bradbury, Whitworth Museum
Alex Britton
Brookbank Day Nursery, Hyde
Derek Brumhead
Circus Tavern
James Cordiner, Manchester Ship Canal Company Ltd
Courtyard Cafe & Penny Farthing Museum, Knutsford.
Disley History Society
Kevin Duffy
Dungeon Pub
Steve England

Fitzpatrick's Temperance Bar
Etrop Grange Hotel & Restaurant
Jane Foster, Arley Hall, Cheshire
Clare Hartwell
David Hilton
Nikita Hooper, National Trust Images
Martin Hughes, The Swan
John Jocys
George Kelsall
Colin Kerron
Andrea Lawless, Wigan Golf Club
Camilla Legh, Adlington Hall
Don Lee
Manchester Evening News
Warren Marshall
Rev Richard and Mrs Lindsay, St George's Church, Mossley
John McConnell, PQ Corporation
Christine McDermott
Chris Makepeace
Ray Makin
Ian Middlehurst
Freda Millett
Anthony O'Grady, Adlington Hall
Steve Orrell, Bury Times
Roman & Maz Piekarski, Cuckooland
Hazel Pryor
Clare Pye, Chairman, Tabley House Collection Trust
Quarry Bank Mill
Andrew Ramshaw, Cheshire East Council
The Romany Society
Rose N Bowl Restaurant
Mark Sheppard
Roy Sharratt
Stalybridge Station Buffet
Glynn Stockdale
Sarah Webb, Tabley House Collection Trust
Vicky Wilby, Tatton Park
Robert Wilson, Automobile Association
John Winn
Mr and Mrs Woodhead

And to anyone else I may have inadvertently omitted.

With special thanks to Cynthia Hollingworth
and Judith Warrender for their diligent proof reading.

Tabley Mere tower

Index

Ashton-Under-Lyne Parish Church